THE FELLOWSHIP OF CHRISTIAN ATHLETES

THE GREATEST LEADER EVER

ESSENTIAL LEADERSHIP PRINCIPLES
FROM
JOHN WOODEN, TOM OSBORNE, TOM LANDRY
JACKIE JOYNER-KERSEE AND MANY OTHERS

Regal

From Gospel Light
Ventura, California, U.S.A.

Published by Regal
From Gospel Light
Ventura, California, U.S.A.
www.regalbooks.com
Printed in the U.S.A.

Dan Britton, General Editor.
Chad Bonham and Shea Vailes, Contributing Editors.
Cover photo of Jackie Joyner-Kersee by Lance Omar Thurman.

Library of Congress Cataloging-in-Publication Data
The greatest leader ever : essential leadership principles / The Fellowship of Christian Athletes.
p. cm.
ISBN 978-0-8307-5920-0 (trade paper)
1. Leadership—Religious aspects—Christianity. I. Fellowship of Christian Athletes.
BV4597.53.L43G74 2011
658.4'092—dc23
2011021713

Rights for publishing this book outside the U.S.A. or in non-English languages are administered by Gospel Light Worldwide, an international not-for-profit ministry. For additional information, please visit www.glww.org, email info@glww.org, or write to Gospel Light Worldwide, 1957 Eastman Avenue, Ventura, CA 93003, U.S.A.

To order copies of this book and other Regal products in bulk quantities, please contact us at 1-800-446-7735.

Contents

What Kind of Leader Are You?

DAN BRITTON

Executive Vice President, Fellowship of Christian Athletes

For God did not give us a spirit of timidity,
but a spirit of power, of love and of self-discipline.

2 TIMOTHY 1:7, *NIV*

Who is the greatest leader ever?

When you throw around the title *Greatest Leader Ever*, everyone has an opinion about who deserves such a prestigious title. You may have picked up this book to find out which leader we have chosen. Throughout history, there have been many legendary leaders who are worthy of consideration. Who would be on your list? Your finalists might be famous trailblazers or possibly just ordinary people who have impacted your life in extraordinary ways.

In order to pick the greatest leader ever, we must first find out what makes a great leader. What are the distinguishing principles, attributes and characteristics that make leaders great? *The Greatest Leader Ever* not only answers the question, "Who is the greatest leader ever?" (yes, we have the answer), but also examines what makes a great leader. Forty outstanding leaders in the world of sports, past and present, will each reveal one essential leadership principle in the following pages. These 40 fundamental leadership principles include qualities such as integrity, respect, faithfulness, love, trust, focus, teamwork and humility. Characteristics such as these define not only the type of leader one is today, but also the legacy one will leave for those who follow.

Before you dive in and enjoy the journey of developing your own leadership capacity, I would like to challenge you with one question: "What kind of leader are you?" I pray that you are a leader of POWER:

Pursue Purity: *A leader of power pursues purity in all things.* Sexual purity is essential, because purity paves the way to intimacy in all relationships. The purity game plan is explained in Psalm 119:9: "How can a young man keep his way pure? By living according to your word" (*NIV*). Purity becomes a lifestyle when you hide God's Word in your heart. The second greatest decision you can make (after surrendering your life to Christ) is committing to be a leader of purity. Pursuing purity is about having right actions, words, thoughts and motives in all areas of your life. A life of purity is one that is marked by excellence.

Obey the Call: *A leader of power obeys the call of God.* God places a call or a mission in each of us, but how we respond is up to us. Leaders of power always respond, "Yes, Lord!" The Lord doesn't try to hide His will from us or make it difficult to know what we should do. Our goal should be the same as David's: "One thing I ask of the LORD, this is what I seek: that I may dwell in the house of the LORD all the days of my life" (Psalm 27:4, *NIV*). When you seek Him, He will reveal what you are made to do. Your gifts, talents and skills can and should be used to glorify Him.

Worship Daily: *A leader of power worships God daily.* Learn when and how to engage Jesus Christ daily. Worshiping God is like breathing. It's not just important—it's mandatory! Discipline yourself spiritually. Paul writes, "Exercise daily in God—no spiritual flabbiness, please! Workouts in the gymnasium are useful, but a disciplined life in God is far more so, making you fit both today and forever. You can count on this. Take it to heart" (1 Timothy 4:7-9, *THE MESSAGE*). Great leaders seek God constantly. Walk with Jesus daily by getting into the Word of God. He is waiting for you to show up.

Engage Others: *A leader of power engages in significant relationships.* According to Proverbs 13:20, "The one who walks with the wise will become wise, but a companion of fools will suffer harm." Find some wise friends and do life together. Most leaders are lonely; they can easily become isolated. Surround yourself with people who want the best for you and who will speak truth into your life.

Reject Apathy: *A leader of power rejects the apathetic spirit and receives from God the spirit of power.* Don't take the easy way out. An apathetic spirit is the *I-Don't-Care* attitude. Leaders need to care. Leaders of POWER approach life as an adventure—not a chore or duty. So, ask the Lord for the courage to be bold and maximize every moment. Proverbs 28:1 states, "The wicked man flees though no one pursues, but the righteous are as bold as a lion" (*NIV*). Ask the Lord to give you the spirit of wisdom to know what's right and the courage to do what's right—even when it is hard. Lead and serve with courage!

Maybe the question should be, "What kind of leader do you want to be?" As you walk through each biblical principle presented in this book, you have an opportunity to grow and change as a leader. Follow the example of the Greatest Leader Ever. Choose to be a leader of POWER today.

1

Leadership Matters

LES STECKEL

President, Fellowship of Christian Athletes

Leading is following in the footsteps of great leaders.

In my 32 years as a coach and my 30 years in the Marine Corps, I learned a great deal about leadership. Even in my post here at the Fellowship of Christian Athletes, I've never stopped growing as a leader. Biblical leadership is truly an ongoing process for me as I continue to build my personal definition of leadership.

Leadership is setting a positive example of integrity, self-discipline, hard work and continually seeking self-improvement. Leadership is knowing your team and looking out for your team members' welfare. Leadership is clearly communicating the goals and objectives that need to be accomplished and understood by the team, and in turn developing a sense of responsibility in your subordinates.

A leader should build relationships founded on integrity and trust. A leader should make timely and sound decisions, always taking responsibility for such actions. A leader should never fear conflict, but should hold people accountable in a professional manner and truly be committed to achieving outstanding results. A leader should never compromise moral, ethical and Christlike values.

The book *Influencer: The Power to Change Anything* tells us that leaders often mimic great leaders and copy the behavior of others they respect.[1] My journey to leadership is a testament to that fact. I have always modeled myself after leaders whom I believe to be great.

To this day, I'm most grateful for my leadership experience in the Marine Corps. The Marine Corps is quite an extraordinary organization. All marines go through the same training no matter their Military Occupational Specialty (MOS). When I finished Officer Candidates School (OCS), the things they stressed the most were physical fitness, mental exams and leadership style. They taught you how to be a leader.

In the Marines, I learned that there are two primary leadership styles. Some leaders are more task-oriented and other leaders are more people-oriented. I wanted to be both. I wanted to accomplish the goal but still be sensitive to people.

I finished 36 weeks of training, and the next thing I knew, I was in Vietnam. Most second lieutenants were given one platoon, but I was given six. Even though it was impossible to be with all of my marines at the same time, I always rubbed shoulders with those six units. I had to get to know who they were, what was important to them and what motivated them.

In 1978, my first year in the NFL with the San Francisco 49ers, I encountered a great leader who would impact my life immeasurably. In the season opener, we played the Dallas Cowboys. As I stood on the sidelines, I think I watched the legendary head coach Tom Landry more than I did the football game. I marveled at his tremendous bearing and demeanor. He exhibited great poise and calmness in high-pressure situations. I said to myself, "I want to be like that." As a young NFL coach, I wanted to model my Christian faith in such a way that I would not bring any shame or embarrassment to our Lord and Savior Jesus Christ.

More recently, during my time here at FCA, I met a man named John Holland. He was the Chief Operating Officer of Fruit of the Loom and, in his mid-70s, came out of retirement to help save the company from bankruptcy. I went to spend time with John to thank him for his contributions to FCA, but selfishly I went to learn from him and seek self-improvement.

I asked him, "What is the key to leadership?"

He said, "Just one thing: self-discipline."

This excited me. I've been a proponent of self-discipline for many years now. But then he asked me to define it. After three failed attempts, John looked at me with a maverick face and said, "Self-discipline is doing what you don't want to do."

That was the greatest definition I had ever heard. When I find myself not wanting to spend time in the gym after driving for six hours, I think back to John's words. That brief time of mentoring taught me that leaders often have to do things they don't want to do and have to make hard decisions that others aren't always willing to make.

Another great example for me was Martin Luther King Jr., whom I believe to be the greatest human leader. He took an almost impossible task and was willing to suffer in a very Christlike way. Leadership requires suffering, sacrifice and surrender. Those are words that most people don't want to have any part of, but Dr. King was that kind of leader. I marvel at what he did for America and the African-American community. I'm so grateful that God raised up a man like that.

But Jesus was unquestionably the greatest leader ever. He displayed such wisdom and stature. His compassion for people was unmatched, and He did everything in perfect timing. Throughout this book you will hear many examples of Jesus' perfect leadership skills. Yet amazingly, we have the ability to lead like the Son of God. The more we allow the Holy Spirit to guide and direct us, the closer we can get to Jesus' level of leadership.

Often our selfish motives can get in the way. When young, aspiring leaders come to me asking for advice, my first question to them is, "Why do you want to be in a leadership position?" People often get caught up in prominence, prestige, popularity, power and positions in life. But before you can become an effective leader, you first must know your purpose in life. Is your attitude selfless in such a way that you want to do the best you can for the group? Is your heart right? Are you where you're supposed to be when it comes to God's perfect will for your life?

To answer those questions truthfully takes an exercise in another of Jesus' great leadership attributes: humility.

Humility is a quality that I greatly respect, but it's also one of the most elusive. Once you think you have it, you've lost it! Pride enters in so quickly. Even when you can feel it coming on, it's still difficult to fight. That's why I always look first to Jesus' tremendous example of humility. Philippians 2:7-8 reminds us, "He emptied Himself by assuming the form of a slave, taking on the likeness of men. And when He had come as a man in His external form, He humbled Himself by becoming obedient to the point of death—even to death on a cross."

Yes, leadership matters. That powerful statement is true in the life of Christ. His leadership has touched millions, perhaps billions of people across the globe. If you are ready to follow in His footsteps, continue reading to learn more about His leadership principles and how they impacted the lives of some remarkable men and women.

TRAINING TIME

1. Who are some leaders that have impacted your life?
2. What are some principles you've learned from those leaders, and how have they made you a better leader?

3. What are some of Jesus' leadership qualities that you most admire? How might those principles change your life as a leader?

PRAYER

Father, I want to lead like Jesus led. I want to be an effective leader for the purpose of Your glory and the advancement of Your kingdom. Help me follow Your Spirit as He guides and directs my steps every day.

Les Steckel is the president of Fellowship of Christian Athletes. He previously coached for 23 years in the NFL. Steckel was head coach of the Minnesota Vikings in 1984 and offensive coordinator of the Tennessee Titans during their Super Bowl XXXIV run in the 1999-2000 season. He also earned the rank of Colonel in the U.S. Marine Corps Reserves, where he served for 30 years.

Note
1. Kerry Patterson, Joseph Grenny, David Maxfield, Ron McMillan and Al Switzler, *Influencer: The Power to Change Anything* (New York: McGraw-Hill, 2008).

2

A Matter of Trust

TOM OSBORNE

Former Head Football Coach, University of Nebraska

Leading with integrity is a matter of trust.

Integrity is a journey; it must stand the test of time.

For me, the road started with a brick. When I was about seven years old, living in St. Paul, Nebraska, I tried to throw a brick onto the roof of our neighbor's house. It came up a little short. Instead of reaching the roof, the brick crashed through the window! When my mom found out what I had done, she marched me over to our neighbor's home and had me confess my youthful indiscretion. Of course it was a rather frightening experience, but one that has stuck with me.

My parents' teaching on integrity and trust began to take root in me and truly sprouted when at age 19 I attended the second annual FCA conference at Estes Park, Colorado, back in 1957. At that conference I made a commitment to follow Christ. Since then I've been blessed to serve as a leader in many different capacities—as an assistant coach, head coach, United States congressman, teacher, athletic director and, most importantly, husband and father.

These roles have taught me that it's impossible to successfully lead others without the presence of integrity in your life. To me, that means you're not one person one day and someone else the next day. Integrity is multi-faceted: telling the truth, keeping promises and maintaining a certain level of consistency. Doing those things engenders a high level of trust, and trust is essential in almost any organization.

The foundation my parents laid proved vital throughout my coaching career. This was especially true in the 1970s and '80s, when college football, in many quarters, was out of control with a good deal of cheating. It certainly wasn't everybody, but there were enough schools doing it that it created an unhealthy environment. Players were being offered clothes, cars and cash. Many schools were devastated by a lack of integrity. This era of corruption culminated in the NCAA-sanctioned "Death Penalty" that forced SMU to shut down its football operations in 1985.

At Nebraska, we lost some recruits to other schools because they were offered incentives that we wouldn't offer. During that period, one of my coaches said to me, "Maybe if we can't beat 'em, we should join 'em."

I think he was halfway jesting, but I answered him seriously: "No, we're going to adhere to our principles." That doesn't mean we were perfect, but we always strived to conduct ourselves that way.

Our confirmation came years later when some sportswriters in Lincoln interviewed 38 former players of mine along with eight assistant coaches for a book called *The Heart of a Husker*. One of the most common things former players and coaches mentioned was their belief that the Nebraska program stood for integrity. Many of them had been promised playing time, starting positions and, in a few cases, some illegal inducements by other football programs.

But at Nebraska, they were simply presented an opportunity. They would have to prove themselves. There were no deals and no promises. There's no question that a few athletes chose not to come to Nebraska because we didn't tell them what they wanted to hear—we told them the truth. We never wanted to give anybody the idea that it was going to be quick and easy or promise playing time. As a result, we built our football program on trust, and leading with integrity is a matter of trust.

Of course, integrity isn't something that suddenly shows up. It takes a lifetime to develop. Integrity is created by individual choices over time. That's why there has to be a certain level of intentionality. People who desire integrity have to evaluate their behavior almost day to day, hour by hour, moment by moment, and revamp the way they operate. As you begin to take that journey, it's sometimes painful. But as you become a person of character and integrity, it becomes a part of you.

Exercising integrity as a leader is actually somewhat freeing. You're not looking over your shoulders much. As conventional wisdom has it, when you tell the truth, you don't need a long memory. Life is much simpler. Relationships will improve because people will gravitate towards you. They'll have confidence in you, because integrity is at your core.

I certainly don't want to give the impression that I'm a perfect person, because like everyone else, I'm fallible. That's why my greatest desire is to be more like Jesus. That should be the goal for all who are called by His name. As I examine His life, I'm continually called to a greater level of integrity.

I am challenged every time I read the Gospels. When Jesus was recasting the Ten Commandments in the Sermon on the Mount, He said, "Let your 'Yes' be 'Yes,' and your 'No,' 'No'" (Matthew 5:37, NIV). Jesus was admonishing us not to use empty phrases to create a false image to others. We have advertising agencies and publicists who specialize in trying to make things look better than they really are. But Jesus, in essence, said, "Don't do that. Just lay it out there and live with the consequences."

Jesus certainly lived that out. When He was before the Sanhedrin en route to the cross, He was asked to renounce His claims that He was the Son of God and the Messiah, but He refused to do so (see Luke 22:66-71). In a way, integrity cost Jesus His very life.

For many years now, I've tried to use Jesus as the model for a life of integrity. My hope is that over time there's been a process of maturing that has led me closer to what He would have me to be—always remembering that no matter what I do, there are times that I'm less than what I should be. But I'm continually called back to a life of integrity as I study Christ's example.

When we examine our lives in the context of who Jesus was and what He did, we realize that sometimes we can lose sight of the overall mission. We make short-term rewards way too important. UCLA coaching legend John Wooden often quoted the philosopher Cervantes, who said, "The journey is more important than the inn."

We focus so many times on the final score or the tangible rewards. But what Jesus emphasized was the process. It's not about the wins and losses. It's about how we play the game. If you keep your eyes fixed on Jesus, winning and losing take care of themselves. He's the "perfecter of our faith" (Hebrews 12:2) and the One who empowers us to lead with integrity to the very end.

TRAINING TIME

1. What does integrity mean to you?
2. What are some consequences you faced when you didn't behave with integrity, and what are some benefits you received because you did behave with integrity?
3. What are the areas where you have gaps in your integrity, and how might you begin to be intentional about closing those gaps?

PRAYER

Father, I want to lead with integrity. Show me the areas where integrity is lacking in my life. Empower me to make right choices every day so that I can develop healthy, trusting relationships with those who are under my leadership.

Tom Osborne is the former head football coach at the University of Nebraska. Over 25 seasons, he led the Cornhuskers to three national championships (1994, 1995 and 1997) and 13 combined Big 8 and Big 12 conference championships. Osborne also served a six-year term in the U.S. House of Representatives. He is currently the University of Nebraska's athletic director. He is the author of *Beyond the Final Score: There's More to Life than the Game.*

Correction, Not Criticism

JOHN WOODEN

Legendary Men's Basketball Coach, UCLA Bruins

Leading sometimes requires corrective discipline.

Criticism and correction differ, especially when it comes to methods and motives.[1] Criticism puts someone down. Correction means I want to help.

Be slow to correct and quick to commend. No one likes correction, but we learn from it. If we commend before we correct, the person will accept the correction better. But we must listen before we correct. There is usually another side to every story. If we listen to others, they will be more apt to listen to us.

It is very important how correction is given. We must be careful how we do it. We don't want those being corrected to lose face. Here are some good tips: Make it meaningful, but use judgment. Don't fly off the handle and be quick to correct. Do it with tact. If we just let it fly, it is more likely to be viewed as criticism than as correction.[2]

You can't antagonize people and then expect to get positive results. I never punished players by making them run laps or do push-ups. I withheld privileges. Discipline was maintained through denying practice time or playing time in games. I don't believe physical punishment is helpful. I didn't want physical conditioning confused with punishment. Early on I made the mistake of antagonizing through physical punishment. Later I learned a better way and, as a result, I became a better teacher.

While I may have occasionally raised my voice, I never yelled at players much. That would have been artificial stimulation, which doesn't last very long. I think it's like love and passion. Passion won't last as long as love. When you are dependent on passion, you need more and more of it to make it work. It's the same with yelling.

Some of my players needed a pat on the back. For others, the pat needed to be a little lower and a little firmer.[3]

Walt Hazzard was a great passer and a fine floor leader, and he understood what I wanted to do, but he tended to be flashy when it wasn't necessary. It wasn't easy to get Walt to give up some of his playground habits. Early in his sophomore year, I benched him against Colorado State, and we lost in double overtime. I gave him three choices: play the game my way, sit and not play, or go someplace else. He decided to quit and called his dad to tell him. His dad talked with him about it. Walt stayed and became one of the best ball handlers I ever coached. His sophomore year, in the semifinals of the Final Four, we lost by two points to the eventual NCAA champions. In his senior year (1964), he was a consensus All-American and played an integral part in our first NCAA championship.

I found the bench to be the greatest ally I had to make individuals comply with what was best for the team. As a result, we lost a few games but developed character in the lives of many young men. We won more championships than any other team ever has, but more important, we developed champions on and off the court.[4]

TRAINING TIME

1. In your station as a leader, what are some examples of the difference between criticism and correction?
2. Which do you struggle with more: resisting the temptation to criticize someone you're leading or comfortably stepping into the role of correcting them? Explain your answer.
3. The line between criticism and correction can be a fine one. In what areas of your leadership can you do better to ensure that your correction isn't turning into criticism?

PRAYER

Father, help me lead with a heart of love. When those in my care need to be corrected, allow me to do so without a critical spirit—first commending and then directing them in the way they should go.

John Wooden was the legendary men's basketball coach at UCLA. Wooden led the Bruins to an unprecedented 10 national championships and a men's college basketball record of 88 consecutive wins. As a player at Purdue, he was a three-time All-American and a key member of the 1932 national championship team. Coach Wooden was a prolific author and penned such classics as *They Call Me Coach, Coach Wooden One-On-One* and *Coach Wooden's Pyramid of Success* (with Jay Carty). Coach Wooden passed away June 4, 2010, at the age of 99.

Notes

1. Excerpt taken with permission from John Wooden and Jay Carty, *Coach Wooden One-on-One* (Ventura, CA: Regal, 2003).
2. Ibid., Day 39.
3. Ibid., Day 38.
4. Ibid., Day 37.

Let Discipline Be Your Guide

JACKIE JOYNER-KERSEE
Olympic Champion, Track and Field

Leading is a test of the will.

If life is a journey, then I believe discipline is our guide. This is true no matter what your goals might be. For me, the goal was to make the improbable leap from the rough streets of East St. Louis, Illinois, to the medal podium at the Olympics. There is no way I could have accomplished such a feat without a strong measure of discipline in my life.

Discipline was modeled to me at a very young age. My mother, Mary Joyner, was a strong believer in discipline. If I wanted to do something, there were certain other things I had to accomplish first. If I wanted to go to the community center or to the track, first I had to make sure my homework was done. Then, I had to make sure my room was cleaned up. If everything was right in her eyes, then I was able to go and do what I enjoyed.

My mother didn't just talk to me about discipline. She showed me what it looked like every day. She got up early in the morning to get ready for work, then caught the bus and made sure she got to her job on time. She always told us she'd be home at 3:30, and she always kept her word. Then, she made sure there was food on the table for us to eat. My mom was a living example of having the discipline to do the small things that make such a big difference.

Discipline is also about respecting other people's time. My mom was a strong believer in that. My coaches would usually pick me up for training, and she didn't want them waiting for me. If they were going to be at our house at a certain time, it was not their responsibility to come to my door to check on me. No, I was supposed to be ready to go before they arrived. That's showing respect for them.

As my career took off, discipline became even more important. I kept a strict routine every day. I was at the track at 7:30 each morning doing my warm-ups before my coach, Bobby Kersee (whom I later married), got there. That helped me get prepared for competitions because I had to be warmed up and ready to go before the race. I had to train for seven to eight hours a day. It was tough to do, but I had to discipline myself to go through that routine every week.

That kind of discipline is the only way to explain how a young girl from a drug-infested community could rise above the distractions and temptations and go on to California, where I would attend UCLA and qualify for four Olympic teams. It took discipline to separate myself from the negativity that surrounded me and not allow myself to fall victim to anything that might pull me away from my dream.

Discipline isn't just important for elite athletes. This key principle is uniquely tied to the success of anyone in a leadership position. In that regard, I think of discipline as a commitment. It's about being punctual, sticking to a schedule and living up to your responsibilities. There are times when your discipline and your will are going be tested. A test could be the loss of a loved one or a physical challenge. When those things come, will you rely on substances or unhealthy relationships to deal with them, or will you stand firm by relying on your faith in God?

I have personally been faced with some difficult circumstances that challenged my discipline throughout my track career. Many people tend to forget that I am an asthmatic. At first, I didn't want to believe that I had asthma. I was considered to be this great athlete, so I wouldn't take my medicine, and because of that, I would become extremely sick. I eventually learned how to be disciplined in my approach to physical health. I had to respect the disease. I couldn't live in denial. I had to take my medicine on a regular basis and do all the things necessary to keep my asthma under control. Discipline became a part of my survival.

I have also experienced great loss. When I was an 18-year-old freshman at UCLA, I had to come back home when my mother became severely ill with a rare form of meningitis and went into a coma. It was up to my brother, Al, and me to decide whether or not to take her off life support. She was just 37 years old when she passed away.

In 1998, tragedy struck our family again when Florence Griffith-Joyner died suddenly after suffering from an epileptic seizure. Florence was known to most as "The World's Fastest Woman" and a three-time Olympic gold medalist, but I knew her best as my sister-in-law and dear friend.

I would never compare myself to Job of the Old Testament, but in some ways I can relate to what he experienced. He dealt with severe physical challenges and lost all of his children to death, yet he never lost his faith. Job never allowed those unfathomable circumstances to knock him off his disciplined life of service to God.

When I was an active, competitive athlete, I couldn't afford to let any obstacle get in the way of reaching my goals. Like Job, I couldn't let my challenges sway me from that disciplined path. Today, I still have a purpose that hasn't been fully revealed, but I know that God is using me as a tool to accomplish something significant. That's why I live each day with the understanding that I don't know what tomorrow is going to bring. As my mom would always say, "Jackie, don't tell me about tomorrow. Take care of today."

For me, taking care of today means staying disciplined. If you're worried about tomorrow, you'll get off that disciplined track and it will be even harder to fulfill God's purpose for your life. As He reveals that purpose to you, it will give you strength to run with discipline and successfully reach the finish line.

TRAINING TIME

1. In what areas do you feel you are well disciplined and in what areas do you lack discipline?
2. How have challenging circumstances tested your discipline? How did you fight through and maintain your discipline?
3. What are some steps you can take to improve those areas that are lacking discipline?

PRAYER

Father, show me the areas of my life that lack discipline and then give me the grace I need to become more consistent. Give me the strength to withstand life's challenges and the wisdom to rid my life of distractions that seek to knock me off this disciplined path.

Jackie Joyner-Kersee is a four-time Olympian, three-time Olympic gold medalist (twice in the heptathlon and once in the long jump), and reigning world record holder in the heptathlon. Joyner-Kersee also won an Olympic silver medal (in the heptathlon) and two bronze medals (in the long jump). She won a combined four gold medals at the World Championships and was named greatest female athlete of the twentieth century by *Sports Illustrated*.

5

Commitment to Excellence

TOM LANDRY

Legendary Head Football Coach, Dallas Cowboys

It's the effort to win that matters.

Vince Lombardi's most famous quote was one he borrowed from an old John Wayne movie in which the Duke played a football coach who said, "Winning isn't everything, it's the only thing."[1] While I'm sure that statement worked well in a rousing pep talk, I don't think it's true. And while I don't doubt Vince used it to make a good point with his players, I don't think he believed it either.

If winning is the only thing that matters, then you'd do anything to win. You'd cheat. You'd sacrifice your marriage and your family to win. Relationships wouldn't matter. People wouldn't matter. Winning would be worth any price you had to pay. I don't believe that; after working with Vince Lombardi day after day for six years, I know he didn't believe it either.

As a competitor, Vince Lombardi had few equals. He hated to lose as much as he loved to win. But a more accurate reflection of his feelings would require a revision of that famous quote. Something like: "Winning isn't everything; it's the effort to win that matters."

We had a quote on a sign in our Cowboy's locker room that said, "The quality of a man's life is in direct proportion to his commitment to excellence." What that means is that you have to get up each morning with a clear goal in mind, saying to yourself, "Today I'm going to do my best in every area. I'm not going to take the easy way; I'm going to give 100 percent."[2]

Having that kind of commitment doesn't guarantee we'll reach our goals. Some of the time we'll fall short. Occasionally we'll hit an insurmountable obstacle and be bounced back off the goalpost like Deacon Dan Towler of the Rams in a 1954 game when he took the ball, lowered his head and charged into the gaping hole behind his teammate Tank Younger. If he'd have looked up he could have waltzed into the end zone untouched. He would also have seen the goalpost, which in those days stood right on the goal line.[3] But no matter what setbacks we might encounter, the determination to strive to do our best will inevitably improve the quality of our lives.

The apostle Paul is one of my favorite biblical characters because he was such a competitor. He was stoned, shipwrecked, imprisoned, and still he wouldn't quit. He explained some of his motivation in a letter to the Corinthian church in 1 Corinthians 9:24-27:

> Do you not know that the runners in a stadium all race, but only one receives the prize? Run in such a way that you may win. Now everyone who competes exercises self-control in everything. However, they do it to receive a perishable crown, but we an imperishable one. Therefore I do not run like one who runs aimlessly, or box like one who beats the air. Instead, I discipline my body and bring it under strict control, so that after preaching to others, I myself will not be disqualified.

Paul understood what it took to be a champion and a successful leader. He realized that the quality of a man's life is in direct proportion to his commitment to excellence.

When I think of people I've seen in my career who embody this truth, I think of Roger Staubach. Twenty-three times he brought the Cowboys from behind to win—14 times in the last two minutes or overtime.

Roger's commitment to excellence improved the quality of his own life and the lives of everyone around him. During his career, the Cowboys went to five Super Bowls. He started as quarterback in four of them, winning two championships. And in the two Super Bowls we lost, Roger was throwing the football into the end zone, giving us a chance to win, as time ran out.

That kind of commitment to excellence—the kind of will to win Paul wrote about—is absolutely essential to successful leadership.[4]

TRAINING TIME

1. Why is winning not everything?
2. What does a commitment to excellence look like in your daily life and sport?
3. How can your commitment to excellence improve the lives of your family, friends, co-workers and teammates?

PRAYER

Father, I commit to a life of excellence for Your glory.
Help me to incorporate excellence into every detail of my daily life,
and help me to improve the lives of those I lead by inspiring
others to live with excellence, too.

Tom Landry was the legendary head football coach of the Dallas Cowboys from 1960-1988. Coach Landry led the Cowboys to a 270-178-6 record, as well as two championship titles in Super Bowl VI and XII, and coached 20 consecutive winning seasons (1966-1985). Coach Landry was admitted into the Pro Football Hall of Fame in 1990, and he passed away on February 12, 2000.

Notes

1. Excerpt taken with permission from *Tom Landry: An Autobiography* (Grand Rapids, MI: Zondervan Publishing House, 1990).
2. Ibid., pp. 287-288.
3. Ibid., p. 103.
4. Ibid., pp. 288-289.

6

Be Available

ANDY PETTITTE

Former MLB Starting Pitcher

Leading requires a desire to build relationships.

I'm not very outspoken. But being the starting pitcher for a World Series champion team inherently forced me, an otherwise quiet, laid-back kid from Deer Park, Texas, into the spotlight. It made me a little uncomfortable at times.

Yet, that was my life as a member of the iconic New York Yankees. In my 13 seasons there, we won five titles and went to two other World Series. I also had the pleasure of playing for my hometown Houston Astros in that franchise's only Fall Classic appearance.

During my time on those teams, like it or not, I was a leader. Because of my position and previous successes—especially in the postseason—other players watched what I did and wanted to know what I had to say. They followed my lead both during and after competition. It wasn't just my job to pitch; it was also my job to build relationships with the other players. You've got to have camaraderie and togetherness on a baseball team if you want to win.

I didn't always understand my responsibility to build relationships with my teammates. When I was younger, even though I was pretty consistent in my walk with the Lord and in sharing my faith, my focus was more on the game. I had so much success early in my career that I became caught in the grind of trying to live up to the high expectations that come with playing in New York.

My perspective suddenly shifted when I left the Yankees to play for Houston in 2004. In the Astros clubhouse, I was one of the older guys on the team. I had a different role. It was almost as if I had become a player-coach. I switched from being so consumed and worried about how I was performing to turning all that over to God and spending my emotional energy encouraging other people and building friendships with my teammates.

It took a torn tendon in my elbow that same season to complete the maturing process. Although I wasn't able to compete for half the season, I had the opportunity to observe my teammates grind it out. That was an eye-opener for me. As I was forced to slow down, I became equipped to build those vital relationships.

I've learned that relational leadership takes the focus off myself and places it on others. When I'm caring about others instead of myself, I find that I'm the happiest and most at peace. You get the benefit of seeing the change in someone's life and enjoying the kind of relationship where someone will come to you and say, "I appreciate that you've been praying for me" or "Thanks for the encouraging words you've given me." There's a special blessing when people trust you and believe you really care for them.

Building relationships isn't easy, but there are some simple things everyone can do to experience the fruit of this principle.

First and foremost, relationship building takes a strong measure of desire. Every year, I went back to my team and specifically prayed about it. I asked God to give me the enthusiasm and the strength to make it through a full season and to do so with the well-being of others in mind. I prayed, "Lord, help me to have the relationships so I can share You with other people." Then I had to make myself available.

The next step requires a proactive approach. Take the time to ask people how they're doing. Ask them how their day is going. Ask about their family. You want to get involved in people's lives. Some will push you away and won't want that kind of interpersonal communication, and that's fine. But it's absolutely amazing what happens when you're consistent in the way you live. When people know that you care about them, and they see that consistent walk, they will share their struggles with you.

Finally, building relationships means letting people know that you care about them and will pray for them. Then you'd better follow up on it. If you say you are going to pray for somebody but never ask about their circumstances, then they'll probably think you're not concerned at all. But if you follow up, your genuineness will mean a lot.

Barnabas is one of the Bible's exemplary models of relational leadership. His name aptly means "son of encouragement" or "son of consolation" (Acts 4:36). Barnabas came alongside Paul, who was recently converted to the faith following his days as a persecutor of Christians, and not only built a relationship with him, but also bridged the gap between this unlikely apostle and the Early Church. What an awesome picture of God's will for relational leadership! As we show love to non-believers and young Christians through our encouragement and availability, we are then able to draw them closer to the knowledge of His saving grace and help them grow in their newfound faith.

Our best example of relational leadership can be found in the life of Christ. I love how He taught His disciples and showed His power to them. Jesus handled them as a great leader building a strong team. He invited them onto the team to achieve one goal: to share His message of hope. Jesus brought them together and had them working in one accord. He wanted to move them in the right direction to achieve the goal.

Jesus was all about relationships. He loved people. He listened to people. He encouraged people. My daily prayer is that I might be more like Christ every day. I want to have that purpose in my life. I want to encounter people with whom I can build relationships so I can share my faith with them and show them God's love. For this quiet, unassuming guy, that is a way I can lead with God's heart.

TRAINING TIME

1. In your leadership position, do you find it easy or difficult to build relationships with those under your authority or those over whom you have influence? Explain.
2. Can you attest to the benefits of relational leadership in your own experience?
3. How might following Jesus' example in building relationships help you improve your relational leadership skills?

PRAYER

Father, give me a love for those whom I lead and those over whom I have influence. Give me boldness and a proactive faith that will allow me to build relationships with others so that I might share Your love and Your message of salvation and hope with them.

Andy Pettitte is a former Major League Baseball pitcher who played for the New York Yankees and the Houston Astros. Pettitte was a member of five World Series champion teams and three All-Star teams. His 19 postseason wins rank as the most in baseball history. He was the second pitcher ever to win the series-clinching games of a Divisional Series, Championship Series and World Series in the same season.

7

Find Your Passion

KURT WARNER

Retired NFL Quarterback and Super Bowl MVP

Leading is less difficult when you love what you do.

One night, my wife, Brenda, and I were out enjoying a good meal together when she asked me, "Why are you the way that you are?" My natural defenses immediately went up, and I answered back, "Why are *you* the way that *you* are?" She actually meant the question as a compliment, not a criticism. She wanted to know how I did so many things in life with passion.

Her question was based on something she had seen on the popular television program *Dr. Phil*. Psychologist Phil McGraw, the show's host, often tells his guests that there are usually ten things that shape a person's life. Our discussion that night made me ponder what had shaped my life.

As I reflected on that question, I was surprised to realize that one of those things was Arena Football. Let me explain. In 1994, I had just been cut from the Green Bay Packers, and I was working in a grocery store. I thought I was too good for Arena Football. I had developed an ego that was telling me, "NFL or bust!" My goal was to attain a life of fame, fortune and worldly success.

The reason I was playing football had changed, and not for the better. I eventually decided to take the opportunity to play in the AFL, and my time there brought me back to my purer motives. There was something in the game that made me feel alive. It's what I call passion!

According to the *American Heritage Dictionary*, "passion" can be defined as "boundless enthusiasm." I love that description. Passion is a burning enthusiasm that emanates from within and has no boundaries. It is a continual longing to quench a certain desire by becoming engrossed in a definitive calling.

As leaders, we must have passion for what we're doing. If we lack longing, those we're leading will sense our half-hearted efforts, and they will likely give us the same kind of lackadaisical performance in return. But before we can show passion, we must know our passion. We can enjoy a lot of things but not have passion for them. There are two ways that we can know for certain that we are passionate about something.

First, you have to gauge the way that activity or role makes you feel. Does it make you feel more alive than other things? Are you energized when you're engaged in your leadership position?

Second, you can know your passion based on how willing you are to give up other things to pursue it. Your sacrifices say a lot about your passions.

When studying this subject, I often substitute the word "love" for "passion," and in 1 Corinthians 13:7, we find one of its powerful byproducts. The apostle Paul tells us that love (or passion) "always perseveres" (*NIV*). In other words, there is never anything that can stop our pursuit of something we truly love.

I remember playing in the annual All-Star football game back in 1989, my senior year in high school. The night before the big game, an individual spoke to all of the athletes about preparing for the future. He told us that of all the great high school athletes in attendance, only 1 or 2 percent would have an opportunity to play professional sports. One of my friends leaned over to me and said, "Wow, what are you going to do?" Although to me it seemed like a rhetorical question, I humored my friend by giving this answer, "What do you think? I'm going to be in that 1 or 2 percent."

My passion has always outweighed the obstacles that I came across. Sure, they were challenging, but they never caused me to reconsider the pursuit of my dreams. There's no doubt that we all face obstacles, but the key is whether our love for something is stronger than anything that stands in our way.

In God's Word there are many great examples of leaders who lived passionate lives: David, Moses, Joseph, Joshua and Caleb, for starters. But few compare to Paul. All you have to do is look through his writings to see how passionate this man was in his pursuit of Christ. Of all the things that characterize his life, few things stand out more than Paul's power to persevere.

In 2 Corinthians 11:23-29, we read that compared to other early Christians, he was "in prison more frequently," "flogged more severely" and "exposed to death again and again" (verse 23, *NIV*). He received 39 lashes (see verse 24). He was "beaten with rods," "pelted with stones" (*ISV*), and shipwrecked three times (see verse 25). He went "without sleep" and was often hungry, thirsty, cold and naked (verse 27, *NIV*). Despite all of these things, Paul continued his labor as a minister of the gospel of Christ.

That is passion. I have met people who have been through some very difficult situations, but I don't know anyone who has endured what Paul suffered. Yet Paul didn't quit. Why? Because his passion for Jesus far outweighed the sacrifices that he willingly made.

But Jesus Himself takes the prize for history's greatest display of passion. In Matthew 27, we read how He was stripped (see verse 28), given a crown of thorns (see verse 29), spit on and struck with a staff (see verse 30), mocked (see verse 31), and finally crucified (see verse 35). Why did Jesus endure all of this? He did it because of His intense passion for you. Romans 5:8 says it best: "But God proves His own love for us in that while we were still sinners Christ died for us!"

It was passion that sent Jesus to earth. It was passion that reverberated through His teachings. It was passion that caused Him to mercifully heal the sick and minister to the poor and downtrodden. It was passion that made Jesus an effective leader to His disciples. And it was passion that gave Him the strength to persevere, even to His death on the cross.

While you and I will never fully understand what Jesus went through, we certainly will face difficulties. Our effectiveness in the face of these obstacles directly depends on our passion for the calling God has placed on our lives. We must understand what we're fighting for, and then let our passion outweigh anything the world throws our way. Only when we experience true passion can we be the effective leaders God has called us to be.

TRAINING TIME

1. What are you most passionate about, and how did you discover this passion?
2. How does passion, or the lack of passion, impact your ability to lead effectively?
3. What steps can you take today in order to ensure that you are actively engaged in pursuing your passion and fulfilling the calling God has placed on your life?

PRAYER

Father, ignite a passion within my heart to fulfill the calling You have given me. If I am not lined up with Your perfect will for my life, reveal to me how I can best serve You and then give me the passion to move forward as an effective leader.

Kurt Warner is a former NFL quarterback who played for the St. Louis Rams, New York Giants and Arizona Cardinals. He was a four-time Pro Bowl selection, two-time AP NFL MVP, a three-time Super Bowl participant, and MVP for the Super Bowl XXXIV champion Rams. He is the author of three books and founder of the charitable organization, First Things First.

8

Prepare for the Game

AVERY JOHNSON
NBA Head Coach

Leading takes a disciplined commitment to training.

Training is what you do in secret. It's preparation for a test, a game or a challenging situation in life.

In the NBA, we have something called training camp, and during the season we hold practices. Those things are done behind the scenes—not when the cameras are on. They're done in secret, but they don't stay secret. What you do in training is going to be exposed in the games.

Training has been a vital part of my development as a player, coach, husband, father and Christian leader. For instance, during my playing days there was a time when I wasn't a very effective shooter. My career was limited and stagnant. I started shooting a thousand shots a day and working with coaches behind the scenes. I had always been a great passer, but once I improved my shot, I became more valuable and received interest from more teams. My salary increased, and then my giving to the Lord increased. That all happened because of training.

On a personal level, my wife, Cassandra, and I have been married for 20 years. We haven't survived that long by luck—or even talent. It's because of what we've done behind the scenes. We've prayed together. We've gone to church together. We've learned problem-solving techniques from other successful married couples. We've been trained in those areas, and because of that, we feel like we have a successful marriage.

From a strictly basketball perspective, my training started at the all-boys St. Augustine High School in New Orleans, where the legendary coach Bernard Griffin taught me about discipline. At Southern University, Ben Jobe taught me to train my mind and my body. My training continued in the NBA, where I played under Gregg Popovich in San Antonio. He took me to another level of discipline and unselfishness. Coach Popovich also taught me how to communicate with my teammates and the importance of keeping my teammates accountable. He taught me how to have a passion, purpose and drive for everything I did on the court.

Training was also vital in my physical development. When I first came into the NBA, I was 5' 10" and probably 150 pounds. Our trainer introduced me to the weight room. If I was going to have a long NBA career, I was going to have to get into that weight room and train my muscles in such a way that I could withstand an 82-game schedule and the wear-and-tear of the travel. At the rate I was going early on, and the way my body looked, I needed to get stronger.

I lifted weights two or three times a week and started training more in the offseason on the track. The training helped give me a mental edge in practice settings and during the games. In addition, because I was in such great shape, I never really got seriously injured. I played in close to 500 straight games. Nobody under six-feet tall has played in more NBA games than I did. Yes, God blessed me, but He also wanted me to do my part. I know that my long career had a lot to do with my training regimen.

Unfortunately, not all athletes share the same passion for training. I've seen many first-round draft picks come into the NBA with a lot of popularity and notoriety. They might be the media darlings of the draft, but they don't last very long in professional basketball because they don't have the proper training. They try to live off their athletic skill, without applying the necessary work ethic.

On the other hand, there are limitations we need to place on our training. There is a danger in putting too much weight on the bar. The same is true in our spiritual lives. If we are trying to lift something that's too heavy—a burden, a trial or someone else's problems—we're really not trusting God. Our training will be negatively impacted. We need to give those extra weights to God so we can run this race in the way He's called us to run it. He has called us to run with passion, desire, responsibility and self-control.

That's why we must lean on the truth found in Proverbs 3:5-6: "Trust in the LORD with all your heart, and do not rely on your own understanding; think about Him in all your ways, and He will guide you on the right paths."

In this microwave age, it's not easy to slow down and train ourselves to trust. Sometimes God wants us to have some quiet, isolated prayer time and devotion time with Him. We need to treat our relationship with God more like an oven. I like to bake. I don't like microwave food. If I'm cooking a steak, for instance, I like to marinate it and turn it over from side to side and make sure it's cooked at the right temperature for exactly the right amount of time. My food is better because I have patience and pay attention to details.

If we have that same deliberate approach to preparation, then when we walk outside our doors into what I call the test or the game, our private training will have an impact in every area of our lives.

Nobody better demonstrated a commitment to secretive, behind-the-scenes training than Jesus. He was the most consistent, relevant example of a leader I've ever seen. From the time He was in heaven with God to His coming to earth and doing all that He did in His 33 years, it was preparation, training, discipline, consistency, commitment and conviction, all wrapped up into one, that made it possible.

That's the example I want to follow. I want to have that same level of commitment so that I might be excellent in everything I do. Then, I will be better prepared to teach those I lead about the priceless benefits of training.

TRAINING TIME

1. What does training look like in your life (physical, spiritual, emotional)?
2. When you're in a game or facing a challenge, what indicators let you know how well trained or prepared you are?
3. What do you need to do today in order to improve your training regimen on all fronts?

PRAYER

Father, give me the discipline to embrace training as a regular part of my lifestyle. Help me to foster an attitude of excellence that will prepare me for the game of life.

Avery Johnson is the head coach of the NBA's New Jersey Nets. He previously was the head coach of the Dallas Mavericks, and in 2006 he led that franchise to its first NBA Finals appearance and won Coach of the Year honors. Johnson spent 16 years playing in the NBA, including as a starter for the 1999 NBA champion San Antonio Spurs.

9

Live for Something More

CLAYTON KERSHAW
MLB Starting Pitcher

Leaders live for something bigger than themselves.

I'll never forget that day: We landed in Lusaka, Zambia, and within a few hours, I was walking in the slums of a local community. I had never seen anything like it. My wife, Ellen, was by my side. This was her fifth time in Africa, and she looked right at home. The streets were quiet. I was overwhelmed by the poverty and filth that surrounded us. Homes made of cardboard, with tin roofs and sheets for windows, lined the street and reached into the horizon as far as I could see.

Slowly, the community came to life. People started poking their heads out of their homes and children came running. I guess it is rare to see Americans in the middle of an African village and even more unusual to see a 6' 4" white man. I stood out like a sore thumb.

Before too long, there was a parade of children behind us. Several ran ahead of us as if to announce our arrival to the next block. One little guy in particular came right up next to me, straining to fall in step with my long stride. I looked down at him, expecting to see a face filled with sadness and despair. But what I saw instead was a boy who was so joyful he burst into a wide grin and a laugh. I wondered how someone who lived in such poverty could have such joy.

Ellen led me to a house that was familiar to her; she knew the family that lived there. We were invited inside, and I did my best not to act surprised by the state of their humble home. Suddenly, I looked down to find a little girl staring up at me. I sat down, and she quickly climbed into my lap. I will remember that moment for the rest of my life. I looked over at Ellen with tears in my eyes. Something she had told me years ago finally came true for me in that moment: When you hold a Zambian orphan for the first time, your life changes forever.

Any ideas I have about being a leader come from the greatest leader ever, Jesus Christ. I came to know Christ as my Savior at a young age. Since then, my walk with the Lord has been the most fulfilling journey of my life. Not even playing in the Major Leagues compares with the richness of knowing Christ. As I strive to be a leader among my peers, on the field, and even in my marriage, I look to Christ as my example.

For many years, Ellen had talked about Africa. She wanted me to see it with her and be a part of what the Lord is doing over there. This past off-season, I finally got to go. Walking in the slums that one afternoon, I was captivated by the pure joy of the children who were running around in ragged clothes, with no shoes. In the Gospel of Matthew, Jesus spends time with little children. He tells His disciples, *"Let the little children come to me, and do not hinder them, for the kingdom of heaven belongs to such as these"* (Matthew 19:14, *NIV*). Jesus sets the example of living for something bigger than ourselves. He is the Son of the Creator of the universe, and yet He took time to love on children.

Throughout His ministry on earth, Jesus lived with one goal in mind: the glory of God. He wasn't concerned with fame and recognition. Jesus' life was about His Father and His mission to redeem God's people. He lived for something so much bigger than Himself. Jesus lived for something more.

As my wife had promised, my time in Africa changed my life. Every evening, I stood on a dirt road outside of the place we were staying and threw a baseball. Children lined the narrow road to watch us play catch. They had never seen a game of baseball. I would spend the last few hours before sunset teaching them how to hold a glove and catch a ball. For the first time, my passion collided with Ellen's. We were in Africa teaching orphans to play baseball.

When we got back to the United States, we decided to do something to encourage people to live for something more. Seeing the Lord at work in Africa changed me. I realized that as a believer and also as a leader, I couldn't allow my life to go on looking the same way it always had looked. I wanted to live for something bigger than playing baseball. Being a leader is about initiating change. Together with Ellen, I wanted to be a part of the Lord's change in Africa.

This season has marked the beginning of "Kershaw's Challenge." For every strikeout I throw this season, we are donating $100 towards building an orphanage in Africa. I want every pitch and every batter faced to be about something more than a game. Jesus led by investing in people and showing them the love of the Father. By God's grace, I want to be that kind of leader. So now, every pitch matters because it is about more than getting to the next inning. It is about the lives of people in Zambia who need food, homes, and most of all, to know the love that the Lord has for them.

It is a struggle to live beyond ourselves. Our culture tells us that life is all about getting ahead, making money and living comfortably. At times, that sounds like a great idea. But in the end, money and fame won't satisfy. Only Christ can fill my life in a way that brings lasting satisfaction. I know that is true for the orphans in Zambia as well. The Lord has blessed me with the gift of throwing a ball, but that gift isn't about me. My marriage isn't about me, and it isn't about Ellen. These good things are about something so much bigger and so much more fulfilling. A godly leader lives in such a way that you notice not the person but the God that person represents.

Leadership involves getting out of the way for God to do great things. It is realizing that we have great purpose right where we are. I love playing baseball. But if life is just about baseball, the journey will be long and empty. This season, the children of Zambia are my inspiration. Winning isn't everything. The Greatest Leader Ever lived for something more. I encourage you to do the same. Is it all about you? How are you living for something bigger than yourself?

As I threw the baseball back and forth with an orphan in Zambia, something I'd heard many times suddenly made complete sense to me: My life is not my own. My favorite passage of Scripture is Colossians 3:23: "Whatever you do, work at it with all your heart, as working for the Lord, not for men" (*NIV*). I hope that whatever you do, you will love it as much as I love baseball. But I also hope that you learn to see your life as a part of something bigger than yourself. Every pitch brings us a step closer to making life better for the children of Zambia. You lead others according to how you live. Live for something big.

TRAINING TIME

1. In order, what are the three most important things in your life?
2. Have you ever had an experience that gave you a new perspective on your purpose? If so, how did it challenge you to live differently?

3. Consider the question, "Am I living for something bigger than myself?" How might answering honestly help you discover what living for something more means to you?

PRAYER

Father, search my heart and reveal to me my true priorities. If they aren't perfectly lined up with Your will, give me the grace and courage to make radical changes in my life so that I might begin to live wholly for Your purpose and make a real difference in my world.

Clayton Kershaw is a starting pitcher for the Los Angeles Dodgers. The team drafted him out of high school in 2006 with the seventh overall pick. Kershaw was *USA Today*'s High School Player of the Year and the Gatorade National Player of the Year following his senior season (during which he posted a 13-0 record and an ERA of 0.77) at Highland Park in Dallas, Texas. Clayton and his wife, Ellen, are the authors of *Arise*, to be released in January 2012.

10

Everybody Has Influence

CHRIS KLEIN
Retired MLS Forward

Leading is a platform.

I became a Christian not long before I became a professional athlete. That was a challenging time in my life. I became more recognizable. I received more affirmation from people. Significant expectations were placed on me. Instantly, I recognized that I had a platform.

That created a conflict for me. While growing up, I always felt like faith was something that was supposed to be very private. Soccer was soccer and church was church and they never intersected. I was unsure how to reconcile the two very differing views within my own heart.

I am thankful that God allowed me the opportunity to start my career in Kansas City. That's where I met Mike Sweeney, who was playing for the Royals at the time. Mike was a very popular person throughout the community. He invited me to study the Bible with him and some other active and retired baseball players. It was a very crucial time in my spiritual growth.

Mike had great influence over me. His discipleship truly shaped much of the way that I approached advancing in my career. He was an intense athlete, but he also loved his teammates and those around him. Mike was very open and bold about his faith. People looked up to him, so his example gave me the freedom to be open about my faith too.

It was through Mike's leadership that I first experienced the power of influence. I now understand that effective leaders need to recognize where they have influence and to what degree. When you figure that out, you can embrace your role and start to build relationships in an effort to impact lives.

That's what I found myself doing early in my professional career. I knew that kids were looking up to me. Teammates were watching the way I led. I was never the guy that jumped down someone's throat or grabbed someone by the shirt. I always tried to encourage people and get to know them and their families. If one of my teammates was having a bad day, I wanted to know why and how I could help. Influence encompasses many leadership qualities—like encouraging, setting an example and serving.

Once I recognized how God made me, the byproduct was a willingness to use my platform. When schools asked me to speak, I said yes, even if it was inconvenient or if I was scared to get up on a stage in front of people. I made a deal with myself that I would say yes to those opportunities.

It didn't take long for me to realize that the fruit of influence isn't always immediate. In fact, you rarely see an impact right away. Sometimes you get instant feedback, but it's usually going to take a while before you see results. I learned quickly that I had to trust God's timing.

On one of my teams, there were some prominent athletes who weren't Christians and were, in fact, very resistant to the faith. I remember speaking to my wife, Angela, about how I'd written them off in my mind. I didn't think I could ever have any influence on them. Angela challenged me on that. She told me to keep being the person God had created me to be. She reminded me that I wouldn't always know God's timing or what He was doing within other people.

A few years later, I had an opportunity to minister to one of those teammates. He came to me and said, "I'm really struggling, and I want what you have." That was the last thing in the world I expected to hear. Yet all along, God was working on his heart.

The biggest gift God gives us is the relationships that come from our life experiences. Now that my playing days are over, it's not the games I miss the most but rather the relationships with my teammates and coaches—that interaction with people who influenced my life and those whom I was able to influence.

That's why Paul is my favorite Bible character. He was a man who had great influence on people close to him, as well as on some individuals that you wouldn't expect. When Paul was in prison, for instance, he didn't hate those who kept him in chains. Instead, he recognized an opportunity to witness to the prison guard, who became a Christian through his testimony (see Acts 16:22-34). That's such a beautiful illustration of influence. A negative situation was completely turned on its head because a prisoner understood the power of God and was given influence in the most unlikely of places.

Paul, of course, was just taking his cue from Jesus, the greatest example of influence known to man. When people gathered around Him, He took those opportunities to speak to them. Jesus told stories and influenced people with His words and His wisdom. He didn't go to the religious leaders so they could in turn influence the people. He went directly to the people. He broke down all barriers and talked with prostitutes, tax collectors, adulterers and the poor. He saw each person, no matter what his or her circumstance, as being worthy of His influence, His time and His love.

In the same way that Jesus used His influence to change the world, we too have the responsibility to use whatever platform, big or small, that God has given us as a means by which we can influence others—through our actions, through our words and through the power of the Holy Spirit.

TRAINING TIME

1. Who has been the most influential person in your life, professionally and spiritually?
2. Who are some people over whom you have influence?
3. What are you doing to make sure your influence is having a positive impact on both those close to you and those who might be watching from a distance?

PRAYER

Father, reveal to me the scope and size of my influence.
Help me understand that my influence may extend beyond people
close to me to include those whom I do not even know. Give me
the grace to walk in Your wisdom and Your compassion so that
I might use my influence to draw people closer to You.

Chris Klein is a retired 12-year Major League Soccer veteran. He ended his career with the Los Angeles Galaxy after previously playing for the Kansas City Wizards, leading that team to the 2000 MLS Cup, and Real Salt Lake. Klein twice overcame major injuries and both times was named MLS Comeback Player of the Year. He also made 25 appearances with the U.S. National Team and scored five international goals.

11

Stay Focused

TAMIKA CATCHINGS
WNBA Forward

Leading a group towards its goal requires intense focus.

I'll never forget my first experience with the principle of focus. When I was in eighth grade, I was flipping through the channels, and Pat Summitt came onto the screen during a women's basketball game. The first thing I noticed about Coach Summitt was the intensity of her eyes. I thought, "This lady's eyes are crazy!"

I put down the remote and my gaze locked onto the screen as I watched, for the first time, the University of Tennessee play. I could see the intense focus in both Coach Summitt and her team. Every player had a purpose. There was no unnecessary movement. You could tell from the coach's eyes what she expected from each one of her players. As an aspiring athlete, that's what I wanted. In that moment, I knew she was someone I wanted to play for.

Since having the opportunity to play for Coach Summitt during my college career, I've learned the true value of focus. This principle is relevant to all leaders, who have the responsibility of concentrating and directing their followers' thoughts and actions in one straight line towards a common goal. A focused leader will get everyone on the same page and keep the team focused on the goal that has been agreed upon.

At the University of Tennessee, our goal was to win a National Championship every year. During my freshman year, I was blessed to have great leaders such as team captains Chamique Holdsclaw and Kellie Jolly as well as the incredibly focused leadership of Coach Summitt. We won the NCAA title that year not just because we were a very talented team, but also because every one of us—from the stars on the court to the role players who came off the bench—was singularly focused on one goal. We refused to allow any distractions to slow us down.

The byproduct of focus is far greater than just winning basketball games or enjoying a prosperous life. Focus allows you to discover your purpose. I was in middle school when I decided I wanted to play professional basketball—even though the WNBA didn't exist yet. I was fixed on that goal, and even though injuries and my parents' divorce were thrown into the mix, my focus has allowed me to play professional basketball here in the United States and around the globe.

Without focus, you lose direction, and ultimately you lose ground. I'm reminded of the story found in Matthew 14:22-33. The disciples were in a boat, in the midst of a storm, when they saw someone walking towards them on the water. Peter said, "Lord, if it's You, command me to come to You on the water."

Jesus told him, "Come." As long as Peter kept his eyes on Jesus, he was able to walk on the water. But when his mind started wandering, and he became fearful of the waves, he took his eyes off Jesus. Peter panicked and began sinking.

I've seen the same scenario play out in my daily life. As long as I'm excited about my Catch The Stars Foundation, and I'm actively working towards reaching our goals, things are good. I'm on solid footing. But as soon as I let fear and doubt enter my mind and begin to worry about our finances or if we're going to have enough kids, then my attitude changes and I lose my focus. My progress eventually grinds to a halt.

It is especially dangerous when a leader loses focus. So often, the loss of focus results in a fall that has far-reaching effects. This is true in sports, business, government and family. All of the people that support the leader and his or her vision are suddenly forced to ask the question, "What are we supposed to do now?" This results in a state of chaos. Even if someone who is well-qualified to lead takes the reins, there is still much uncertainty among the team, and trust becomes a very real issue.

So what, then, are some ways a leader can stay focused? Personally, I've found journaling to be one of the most effective tools. If I have a lot of things to accomplish, I'll sit down and write a to-do list, and then I'll prioritize the items on the list. If you're overwhelmed about how to tackle all of your projects and try to do everything at once, you'll end up getting nothing done.

Another practical tip for staying focused is to be mindful of the people you allow into your inner circle. I preach a lot to kids about how they need to pick their friends. Don't let your friends pick you. That's one thing my dad told me early on. In seventh grade, when I decided I wanted to be a professional basketball player, I had to make the choice to spend my time on homework and practice instead of going to the mall with a group of friends or staying out on the street after the lights went out and I was supposed to be home. If I had made the wrong choices, I would have lost focus on my goal.

The higher you get in the world, the more people are going to want to get close to you and enjoy the ride with you. You must figure out their true motives for being at your side. That's why I have four close friends that I can call at any time. Kids must make sure that the people they're hanging out with are helping them reach their goals by keeping them focused.

Another way I stay focused is through principled daily devotions. I stay in the Word. That's where I learn more about the disciplined focus that Jesus displayed throughout His life. The Bible tells us that He woke up early every morning and made sure to talk to God one on one without any interruption. To do that, He had to be focused. It would've been easy for Jesus, with so many people hanging around Him and demanding His attention, to do it later or put it off. But His focus was on starting His day in communion with God.

Christ's example demonstrates the kind of focus all leaders must have to achieve the purposes for which God created us. That's the kind of focus I must have in my life; I want people to see it in my eyes.

TRAINING TIME

1. What are the things that you most often find yourself focused on throughout the day? Are those things lined up with your goals and purpose, or are they really just distractions?
2. Why do you think it's important to know your purpose and to set goals?
3. What are some of the distractions in your life that you need to get rid of in order to improve your focus and ultimately reach your goals?

PRAYER

Father, help me stay focused on what matters most to You. Shield me from the distractions that bring chaos and confusion into my life. Give me the wisdom to recognize and rid myself of anything that keeps me from fulfilling Your purpose.

Tamika Catchings is a WNBA forward who plays for the Indiana Fever. She is a four-time WNBA Defensive Player of the Year and two-time Olympic gold medalist. Catchings was named WNBA Rookie of the Year in 2002 and was an All-American and member of the 1999 NCAA championship team at Tennessee. She is also the founder of the Catch The Stars Foundation, a mentoring program for young people in Indianapolis.

Finish the Race

RYAN HALL

Olympic Marathoner

Leading is a test of endurance.

In athletics, the marathon is often considered to be synonymous with the word "endurance." From my perspective as a professional long-distance runner, I wouldn't argue otherwise.

My personal definition goes something like this: "Endurance means putting one foot in front of the other no matter how things are going." When running a marathon, there's no avoiding the rough patches when your mind and body start to conspire against you. I've had to develop a process of mentally coaching myself through those difficult parts of the race and pushing through them to the finish line.

The marathon is also a good analogy for life in general. You will go through circumstances that cause you not to feel your best physically or emotionally. You can get down on yourself or, even worse, cave in and give up. Those are the times when you have to encourage yourself to keep moving forward towards the promise of a better tomorrow.

I really love talking about the marathon as it relates to the spiritual realm. I believe that endurance is finishing the race that God has set before us. Endurance is the understanding that we must not give up until we have accomplished the purpose for which we were destined.

For me, the race analogy for endurance is quite literal. I first discovered this principle when God inspired me to go for a run around Big Bear Lake in my California hometown. I was only 14 and had yet to begin my career, but on that day I believe the Holy Spirit showed me that my destiny was to be one of the best runners in the world and to reach others for the kingdom of God.

Over time, I've learned many valuable lessons about the keys to endurance. Perhaps most important is the fact that physical and mental endurance are equally necessary. The two go hand in hand, and both require a lot of hard training. There's no easy way to suddenly be physically and mentally fit enough to compete with the best marathon runners in the world. It's a daily process involving gradual improvement. There's really no other way around it, and there are certainly no shortcuts.

Endurance also means getting up when you fall and moving past your mistakes. This is true both physically and spiritually. I can try my best as a runner and as a Christian, but there are times when I mess up and fail. It's easy to get down on myself, but I've learned over time to pick myself up off the ground and avoid the temptation to slow down.

That's why one of my favorite verses is Proverbs 24:16: "Though a righteous man falls seven times, he will get up, but the wicked will stumble into ruin." To me, Solomon's observation perfectly illustrates the concept of endurance.

Another key to endurance is rest and recovery. There have been times when I was at the end of a season and I was really excited about the way things had gone. Instead of taking the necessary time to recover, I kept going without a break. I learned the hard way that if I ignore the principle of rest within the cycle of endurance, it will always come back to haunt me.

Rest is a recurring theme in God's Word. He set forth that principle at the time of creation, when He took a break on the seventh day. Our bodies are designed to work and then rest. You can't skimp on that recovery time, otherwise your body won't adapt to the next cycle of training. It's easy to want to leave that part out. You can get the mentality that you just want to work harder, but recovery is vitally important to your endurance.

There is no way I could truly endure the physical and mental stress of long-distance running without the spiritual inspiration I receive from my relationship with Jesus. Before all of my big races, I like to watch *The Passion of the Christ* because that's an amazing picture of how Christ went through so much for us. I think about His motivation and what it must have been like for Him to endure that type of pain for such a long time. It puts the pain I experience as a runner into perspective. I'm reminded that what I do isn't that big of a deal in comparison.

Jesus was all about finishing the race set before Him. He endured the cross so that we could enjoy an eternal prize at the end of our journey here on earth. Remembering what Jesus did for us and fixing our eyes on that prize are ultimately what enable us to endure things that we never thought we could possibly survive.

That's how Paul, who endured great hardship for his faith and was martyred for following Christ, was able to write these words: "I have fought the good fight, I have finished the race, I have kept the faith" (2 Timothy 4:7).

Just like running a marathon, being leaders requires us to exhibit a significant measure of endurance. Our minds and our bodies must both be strong. We must train hard and stay disciplined in the ways of God's Word. We must also take time to rest in Him and allow for spiritual recovery and renewal. When we stumble and fall, we can't stay on the ground for an extended time or, worse, give up on our destiny.

Your calling may not be to run races, but in the same way that God inspired me to use my talents and gifts to share the gospel, so too have you been called to lead others to Christ through whatever platform upon which He has placed you. By His strength and grace, we can all endure the challenges of this life until we cross the finish line into eternity.

TRAINING TIME

1. Can you think of a time when you had to endure hardships en route to accomplishing your goals? How did it feel when you finally "crossed the finish line"?
2. How does endurance (physical, mental and spiritual) factor into your life as a leader?
3. Think of a situation in which you've been tempted to give up. How can you start to lean on God's strength and grace to help you keep going until your destiny has been fulfilled?

PRAYER

Father, grant me supernatural endurance so that I might run this race to the finish line. I pray for encouragement from Your Holy Spirit to help me through the rough patches of life. Give me the grace to get back up when I fall and the strength to keep moving forward.

Ryan Hall is an American long-distance runner who holds the U.S. record in the half marathon and was the first American to break the one-hour barrier. He holds the fastest marathon time among U.S.-born citizens and finished tenth at the 2008 Beijing Olympics. While attending Stanford University, Hall won the NCAA Championship in the 5,000-meter race.

Don't Deviate

SHAUN ALEXANDER

Retired NFL MVP Running Back and NCAA All-American

Leading with an unwavering spirit will impact others forever.

It was the summer before my sophomore year at Boone County High School when Owen Hauck, one of the greatest coaches in the history of Kentucky football, walked into the locker room.

Coach Hauck always gave a speech to the sophomore class as they prepared to take their place in the winning football program. It was finally my turn to learn from this living legend.

His words were strong, sincere and focused. He spoke about carrying on tradition, playing hard and winning. He ended his speech with these words:

"We have great coaches here, and they will put you in a position to be the best and be a champion, but you must do one thing: Play all out until the final horn blows."

As he walked out of the locker room, he stopped at the door, turned around and said something I will never forget:

"Boys, the way to the top is straight. Don't deviate!"

Coach Hauck knew something about the way to the top. In 18 years at Boone County, he won 12 District Championships,

10 Regional Championships and one State At-Large Championship. He taught us never to deviate from the game plan. Coach Hauck encouraged us to be ourselves and do what we do best. He taught us what it meant to have an unwavering spirit.

I carried that principle throughout high school, college and the NFL. If you ask any of my former teammates, they'll all tell you the same thing: "Shaun wants to score all the touchdowns." It's funny to say, but it's really true. I believe that everyone on the team has a role. My role was to score points. My workouts, practices and pre-game routines were all in preparation to do that one thing.

Scoring touchdowns wasn't my identity. Scoring touchdowns was my role. It was my calling. I was unwavering about my job. I thank coaches and teammates for being patient with me as I learned to mature and work at doing other things. I know I drove them crazy at times, but I also know they loved the fact that if a touchdown was needed they could always count on me to want the ball.

I've been blessed to have some great leaders, Coach Hauck among them, in my life. They have inspired me to duplicate some of the great leadership attributes they modeled. One of the principles I learned from all of them was how to lead with an unwavering spirit. To do so requires three vital things: (1) know who you are; (2) know what you believe; and (3) fearlessly live out your calling.

I can't think of many better examples of an unwavering leader than the biblical prophet Elijah. He had a dramatic, passionate desire to teach and prove that his God was the one true God. In 1 Kings 18:16-40, we read about a time when God had caused a drought throughout Israel because of the wicked King Ahab. Elijah called on the king and the people of Israel to stop worshiping other gods. He boldly asked, "How long will you waver between two opinions? If the LORD is God, follow him; but if Baal is God, follow him" (verse 21, *NIV*).

Elijah then challenged 450 of Baal's prophets to pray for their god to bring fire from the sky and burn up their sacrificial altar.

They prayed to their god, sang to their god, danced for their god, cut their arms and bled for their god, but nothing happened. Elijah mocked the false prophets and then prepared his own altar. He even had 12 jars of water poured on the wood and the animal sacrifice.

After Elijah offered a passionate prayer (see verses 36-37), God burned up the sacrifice, the wood, the stones and the soil— the flames even licked up the water. Elijah was unwavering in his belief. Even if he was the only one to believe when all the odds were stacked against him, he was not going to falter in his stance.

We see that same unwavering leadership in the life of Jesus Christ, who is hands-down the greatest leader ever. He never shirked His responsibilities. He never hesitated when making decisions. He never faltered in His integrity and the way He lived His life. That's because Jesus knew who He was, knew what He believed and fearlessly lived out His calling. That calling was to go to the cross and give up His life to bring salvation to sinners.

He could have taken an easier road. He could have avoided the pain and suffering. As the crucifixion drew close, the disciple Peter tried to stop Roman soldiers from capturing Jesus. Peter grabbed his sword and cut off the ear of one of the soldiers. But Jesus rebuked Peter and said, "Do you think that I cannot call on My Father, and He will provide Me at once with more than 12 legions of angels? How, then, would the Scriptures be fulfilled that say it must happen this way?" (Matthew 26:53-54). No, Jesus never wavered. He didn't deviate from the plan.

I have been attracted to that unwavering spirit ever since I first accepted Christ as my Lord and Savior, on Easter Sunday, when I was 10 years old. That was the beginning of my own unwavering journey. I am just as committed to Jesus today as I was back then. I haven't been perfect. I've stumbled and sinned along the way, but God's grace has always forgiven me, picked me back up and given me the strength to move forward. In the Old Testament,

God instructs Joshua: "Be strong and very courageous. Be careful to obey all the law my servant Moses gave you; do not turn from it to the right or to the left, that you may be successful wherever you go" (Joshua 1:7, *NIV*).

That is the epitome of an unwavering spirit, and God wants us to have the same strength, courage and refusal to deviate from His ways. Like Coach Hauck said, "The way to the top is straight." That's why I'm so determined to follow his advice from my sophomore year and the advice found in Joshua 1:7. Know your role, know the plan and don't deviate!

TRAINING TIME

1. What are some examples of leaders that you believe had (or have) an unwavering spirit?
2. Where do you find your leadership to be the most unwavering? In what areas do you struggle to stick to the plan?
3. What aspects of Christ's life might give you the strength and the inspiration to be unwavering?

PRAYER

Father, I want to lead with an unwavering spirit. Never let me forget who I am in You. Remind me daily of my calling. Give me the strength to fearlessly pursue the plan You have laid before me.

Shaun Alexander is a retired nine-year NFL veteran who spent most of his career with the Seattle Seahawks. He was a three-time Pro Bowl selection and both the NFL MVP and Offensive Player of the Year in 2005. Before an All-American career at the University of Alabama, Alexander was the top-ranked high school player and Kentucky state record holder with 54 touchdowns in 1995. He is the only player ever to have 100 touchdowns in high school, 50 in college and 100 as a professional.

14

Be Faithful in All Things

CLINT HURDLE

Manager, Pittsburgh Pirates

Leading faithfully produces reciprocal blessings.

I must confess, for many years I treated Jesus Christ like an ATM card. I only pulled Him out of my back pocket when I needed something. I attended church from the age of seven but didn't make a declaration of repentance until I was in high school. Even then, I wasn't faithful; I had no idea what it meant to be faithful to God.

That all changed when I turned 40 and realized I needed to reconnect with God if I was going to be the best person, husband, father, friend and leader I could be.

I've come to understand that God doesn't ask us for many things. One thing He does ask of us, though, is our faithfulness. Jesus says that if we're faithful to Him, He's going to bless us (see Matthew 25:14-30). He doesn't explain how He's going to bless us. He just tells us He's going to bless us. To me, the trust part of that relationship—the fact that we can depend on the unconditional love that He has for us—is eye opening, rewarding and challenging.

While I'm still learning every day what it means to be a faithful Christian leader, I have discovered a few ways that we can express our faithfulness to God. Most of them are relational and have everything to do with the way we treat people—from those closest to us to the strangers whose paths just happen to cross ours.

Each morning, before my feet hit the floor, I make a commitment to live by the Golden Rule that Jesus teaches in Luke 6:31. I need to treat others the same way I want to be treated. That requires a true servant's heart and understanding in everything I say and do.

The challenge is to realize that life's not all about you. That's hard. I don't think it happens overnight. But I've come to understand that we truly live our best lives when we get outside of ourselves and serve others. Our team plays its best baseball when we play unselfishly. My relationship with my wife is so much better when I serve her. My relationship with my family is better when I keep my kids high on my priority list and make time for them.

I'm here to serve God in whatever capacity He chooses to use me each and every day. The ups and downs are always going to be there, but they are momentary when you line them up against eternity. They may seem long when you're going through them, but they look much shorter if you remember that you're being judged from above. I'm not ultimately being judged by a news journalist or by the fans. I can't control things outside of my relationship with Christ and the way I treat other people, so the ups and downs that come with the world of sports have to be let go.

Another way I can be faithful to God is by sharing His love and truth with the world. There are a lot of tools available to us to help share the gospel with others, but nothing speaks more loudly than our actions. Being vocal is a good tool and a good way to bear witness to who Christ is, but you have to back your words up with action. You can pick up the paper every day and read about people who talk about doing right but don't. Our actions prove or disprove our words. The power of the spoken word when it's backed up by action becomes very significant.

I've also found that faithfulness to God will manifest itself as you become involved in a community of believers. One of the most dangerous situations anybody can get into is isolation. If we want to remain strong, scripturally and spiritually, we need to be plugged into something larger than ourselves. Even Jesus, the Son of God, sought out help and surrounded Himself with a group of people He could teach, nurture and train to become a powerful band of Christian leaders. When He faced His greatest trial, He asked His closest friends to pray with Him (see Matthew 26:38).

Finally, faithfulness means not letting negative opinions sway you from the task at hand. When I was the manager at Colorado, we were routinely criticized by some members of the media who weren't comfortable with the strong Christian element within the front office and in the clubhouse. I've often been asked how I handled the attacks. Number one: I didn't get caught up in the controversy. Number two: I loved the ones who were criticizing us. Number three: I didn't really care what they had to say. They didn't know me, and they probably didn't know our organization. They were simply stating their opinions. Everybody's entitled to an opinion. It was up to me to decide whether or not I was going to let those opinions keep me from being the leader I knew God wanted me to be.

It took me far too long in life to stand up for something, so now I've decided it's time to make that stand. I believe in what I stand for with all my heart. Pleasing God is what's important to me. I don't make choices out of an attempt to get applause or a high rating in a Gallup poll. Those things are insignificant factors in my quest to be faithful to God.

Faithful Christian leadership takes on even greater meaning when held up to the standard set by Jesus. There has never been, and never will be, a greater model of faithfulness than Christ. He was faithful to His mission. He was faithful in His attitude of loving kindness to everyone—even those who despised Him. He was a faithful servant to the poor and a faithful healer of the sick. He was faithful even though the religious leaders of the day criticized Him and called Him a liar. He was a faithful friend to His disciples, regardless of the fact that in their humanity they weren't always faithful to Him.

Jesus continues to be faithful today. In Philippians 1:6, Paul writes, "I am sure of this, that He who started a good work in you will carry it on to completion until the day of Christ Jesus." That's good news for all of us who have made the decision to follow the road He has already traveled.

As Christian leaders from every walk of life, we must take Jesus out of our back pockets and be faithful in all things—not just to reap the blessings that God faithfully gives, but also so we can bless others and be an example of faithfulness to a world that desperately needs the hope of salvation.

TRAINING TIME

1. What are some ways God has been faithful to you, and how have you been faithful to Him?
2. What are some areas of your life where you've struggled in your faithfulness to God?
3. As a leader, how do you think your faithfulness to God can influence those who follow you?

PRAYER

Father, thank You for Your faithfulness to me even in those times I haven't deserved it. Give me the strength and grace to be more faithful to You every day. Show me the places where I've struggled in my faithfulness and teach me how to make every part of my life a testament of my love for, and devotion to, You.

Clint Hurdle is the manager of the Pittsburgh Pirates. He previously managed the Colorado Rockies and led that franchise to its first National League pennant in 2007. As a player, Hurdle spent 10 years at the Major League level playing for Kansas City, Cincinnati, St. Louis and the New York Mets.

15

Know Your Role

MIKE JARVIS

Head Men's Basketball Coach, Florida Atlantic University

Leading is just one small piece of a much larger picture.

As a young basketball player at Northeastern University, I thought that I was always the one that should make the game-winning play. As a coach, there have been times when I've felt very confident in my command of the *X*s and *O*s and believed that anything I did was going to be successful. But God has given each of us different abilities to fulfill varying roles in order to achieve a specific goal. I've learned that I am just one part of a bigger picture.

When I was a college sophomore, I quit the team because I thought I was better than I was, and I was certain I knew more than the coach. I was wrong. Sure, I had talent, but I didn't have a good grasp of the fundamentals, and my talent was more limited than I thought. Fortunately, my coach took me back and gave me another chance. I was eventually named captain of the third-string defensive team. Our job was to practice hard, play defense and get the team ready for the game. I soon realized that our role was just as important as the first and second teams' roles.

But I still had some hard lessons left to learn. In 2003, my coaching career at St. John's University was going very well. We had just won the National Invitational Tournament. I had been given a part in a movie. I had co-authored a book. I was in contract negotiations for a substantial salary increase. I really thought I was in control.

Then, after a rough start to the 2003–2004 season, I got a call from my attorney telling me the powers that be at St. John's did not want me there and were interested in talking about a buyout. At that moment, things became clear to me: *You're good, but you're not as good as you think.*

Sometimes we have to be knocked to our knees before we start to look up. God has to take us to the lowest places. Otherwise, we would never get to the highest places. That's when I went back to the basics as a coach. I had to look at my real purpose and reason for getting into coaching. I didn't get into coaching to get rich and famous. I got into coaching to try to make a difference in the lives of players who were, in many instances, just like I used to be.

When my coaching career picked back up at Florida Atlantic, I was able to look into my past and gain inspiration from Tom "Satch" Sanders, the head coach at Harvard University back in the early 1970s. I had the privilege of serving as his assistant coach from 1973 to 1979. Coach Sanders set a powerful example of embracing your role.

Satch was a member of eight Boston Celtics NBA Champion teams between 1960 and 1969. Even though he was a First Team All-American out of New York University, Satch's role during all of those years was to be the defensive stopper. He covered the other team's best offensive players. Very seldom did he get opportunities to score. After a while, he didn't even care about that. Satch understood his role and wholeheartedly embraced it. He was an instrumental part of the Celtics' success. You can't win championships without role players like Satch Sanders.

Having players who understand their roles is a vital key to success for any team. This fact is illustrated by the apostle Paul in 1 Corinthians 12:12-26, where he compares the physical body to the Body of Christ. "For as the body is one and has many parts, and all the parts of that body, though many, are one body—so also is Christ" (verse 12).

Paul goes on to describe a humorous scenario where different body parts argue their supremacy over other parts, but then lays the debate to rest: "Instead, God has put the body together, giving greater honor to the less honorable, so that there would be no division in the body, but that the members would have the same concern for each other" (verses 24-25).

Just like our body parts each serve a distinct function, every member of a team—from the head coach down to the last player off the bench—has a role to play in the achievement of the team's goals. That's why I make sure to praise my players for doing the little things like taking a charge or blocking out. I demand those things from my players. There are many opportunities during practice for you to develop the roles that each team member is supposed to have, whether on offense or defense.

There's no greater model of this principle than Jesus—the greatest leader of all time. At any point during His time on earth, He could have said, "You know what, I'm not going to carry this plan through to fruition. I'm going to end it now. I don't have to deal with this." But He knew that if He didn't perform His role, then none of us could experience salvation.

Jesus also taught the principle of knowing your role by the way He interacted with His disciples. He made it clear to each of them that they had specific strengths. He gave some of them nicknames. He called Peter "The Rock." That would be like me calling someone on my team "Rocky" in a positive way to highlight that person's strength. Then Jesus allowed the disciples to do what they did best. He allowed them to play their roles.

Everybody needs a head coach. Everybody needs a leader. Our leader is God the Father, God the Son, and God the Holy Spirit. Each of us needs to be in daily communication with our leader. In my case, it's the first thing I do in the morning. I want to make sure I'm in the Word and that I'm getting fed. Everything we need to know about our role as leaders and the roles of those we are leading has already been put in God's playbook for us. Follow that, and we'll be in the role God has called us to fill.

TRAINING TIME

1. What are some things you are responsible for in your current role as a leader?
2. Have you ever stepped outside of that role and tried to take on more responsibility than what you had been given? Or, have you resisted taking on some of the responsibilities that are part of your role? What were the results?
3. What are some ways you can better embrace your leadership role?

PRAYER

Father, help me to understand, accept and embrace the role You have given me to fill. Give me the patience and grace to work within that role and to help those I lead to feel comfortable and valuable in their roles.

Mike Jarvis is the head men's basketball coach at Florida Atlantic University. He has also been the head coach at Boston University (where he was the 1990 America East Coach of the Year), George Washington and St. John's. Jarvis has collectively taken his teams to nine NCAA Tournaments including two Sweet 16s and one Elite Eight appearance. He is one of just four NCAA Division I coaches to have won 100 games at three different schools.

16

My Life Isn't Mine

DANNY WUERFFEL

Retired NFL Quarterback and Heisman Trophy Winner

Leading with authenticity takes disciplined selflessness.

Of my three kids, two are boys—Jonah and Joshua. Their favorite thing to do is play with little toy cars. Over the past several years, they've accumulated quite a collection. They'll go into their rooms to play cars, and for a while both are happy. They might have several hundred cars to play with, but without question, they end up arguing over one car. They usually start screaming one word to each other: "Mine!"

It's kind of funny when they're two or three years old, but what about when they're 10 or 20 or 40 years old? We adults might not run around like my kids screaming "Mine!" over toy cars, but when we look at the way we live our lives and invest our time, money and talents, we come to realize that we are in orbit around ourselves.

But, "It's not about you"[1] (or me). Those famous first words of Rick Warren's bestseller, *The Purpose Driven Life*, speak volumes about our tendency to focus on ourselves. While this modern-day classic was never labeled a leadership book, the concept of selfless servanthood is certainly a principle by which every great leader must live.

The problem, however, is that at the core of our beings, we are self-absorbed. That's why we each have to constantly remind ourselves, "My life isn't mine. It belongs to God, and only what I accomplish in His name will matter in the end."

Learning this principle of selfless leadership is something I must purpose to embrace daily. When I was younger, I wasn't intentionally pursuing this principle, but from time to time opportunities for generosity or self-sacrifice presented themselves. When I was in the second grade, I bought a drink from a vending machine. There was another boy there who also wanted to buy something but didn't have enough money. I vividly remember how sad he was. Remembering that I had a little extra change, I combined what I had with his money, and he was able to get a drink. The joy he experienced from that simple act of kindness, and the thankfulness he expressed, made me feel wonderful.

There's no doubt that my first example of selfless leadership was my mother, an extremely talented woman. She was musically gifted; she could sing like an angel and play numerous instruments. At one point, she had the opportunity to pursue a music career but chose instead to be a wife and mother. She gave of herself, investing her time and talents in her kids. Without question, her sacrifice made a huge difference in my life.

In 2003, I was working out with the New Orleans Saints as a free agent. My process of understanding life through a biblical worldview caused me to look at things differently and try to see where God might be opening doors for me. I was looking for opportunities, asking Him to show me where I needed to invest my life. I had no idea what those opportunities might be, but I was keeping my eyes open. That's when I started volunteering at Desire Street Ministries—an outreach to New Orleans' Lower Ninth Ward. The people there captured my heart. It was a natural transition to retire from football and start working full-time in a leadership capacity at Desire Street.

Even as God's grace has led me this far, I still understand the counterintuitive nature of this leadership principle. It's not natural. People are self-absorbed, and servant leadership is something that has to be taught and practiced. For every generation, parents and leaders have to set the example and make it a priority. Right now for our young children at home, my wife and I have three things we try to say over and over: We love Jesus, we love to have fun and we love to help people.

In so many ways, popular culture runs counter to God's Word. This is especially true when it comes to servant leadership, one of the Bible's underlying themes. One of my favorite verses is James 1:27: "Pure and undefiled religion before our God and Father is this: to look after orphans and widows in their distress and to keep oneself unstained by the world."

James refers to two things in his definition of religion. One is that we are to keep ourselves from being stained or polluted by the world. That tends to be what most of us think is the totality of religion: growing in righteousness. But he also tells us we are to look after widows and orphans. That is a key part of what authentic religion is about. Widows and orphans in that day were the most vulnerable members of society; they were most susceptible to being mistreated, and they had great needs. For us today, our relationship with God should compel us to minister to the hurting, the suffering and those with great needs.

I am also challenged by a passage in Jeremiah where God says about King Josiah, "He took up the case of the poor and needy, then it went well. Is this not what it means to know Me?" (Jeremiah 22:16). So much of our energy as Christians goes toward knowing God. If God's heart for the poor is as central to His nature as I believe it is, then there are aspects of God's heart that we may not be able to know unless we are participating in selfless leadership.

We need look no further than the life of Christ for the perfect example of selfless leadership.

The totality of His life and mission exemplifies serving others. I'm reminded of 2 Corinthians 8:9, where Paul says, "For you know the grace of our Lord Jesus Christ: although He was rich, for your sake He became poor, so that by His poverty you might become rich." He has given all of Himself so that we can have all the things He deserves as the Son.

Jesus lived out this principle beautifully when He got down and washed the feet of the disciples. They didn't want Him to do that, but He came to serve. He didn't just give up His time or His talent or His riches in the Kingdom. He gave up everything. He gave Himself. He gave His life for us.

Christ's example shows me that there is a different game going on. There's a different race happening that we can't see, but its results will last for eternity. Being a servant leader means having an eternal perspective, rather than a short-term perspective, on how to live life—a life that doesn't belong to us but rather belongs to the One who saved us.

TRAINING TIME

1. What do you find most challenging about maintaining a selfless life?
2. You may be willing to serve, but how do you react when someone treats you like a servant?
3. What are some ways you can naturally begin to incorporate selflessness into your leadership style?

PRAYER

Father, give me a selfless heart. Give me the courage to step outside of my fears and my selfish desires so that I might be an example of Christ's servant leadership to those whom I am able to influence.

Danny Wuerffel is a former NFL quarterback who played for the New Orleans Saints, Washington Redskins, Green Bay Packers and Chicago Bears. At the University of Florida, Wuerffel led the Gators to the 1996 National Championship and was the 1996 Heisman Trophy winner. Wuerffel is now the executive director of Desire Street Ministries, www.desirestreet.org.

Note
1. Rick Warren, *The Purpose Driven Life* (Grand Rapids, MI: Zondervan, 2002).

Operate in Truth

JANE ALBRIGHT

Head Women's Basketball Coach, University of Nevada

Leading with truth and love is a winning combination.

As a leader, you should be willing to set the bar very high. That doesn't mean you have to be perfect, because leadership isn't about what you do—it's about who you are. It can't be based upon appearances. To be an effective leader, you must have a heart that seeks truth.

In order to lead people, you have to paint the vision, and at the same time know where each team member is on the journey. Sometimes you have to say hard things to a young person. It might be something like, "Sally is a better basketball player right now than you are, and that's why she gets to play more minutes." After you've spoken the truth to your players, you can begin to work on those areas where they need to improve.

Those you lead also have to understand that truth needs to be reciprocal. I've had years of experience with players who have told me things that weren't true—and we ended up going to a place where we never should have gone. Yet, if I gathered my players and asked them if they considered themselves to be liars, none of them would raise their hands. If I asked them how many had told a lie today, most of them would probably tell me that they had. We have a serious disconnect between truth and deceit.

Growing up in Graham, North Carolina, a small town between Greensboro and Chapel Hill, I was expected, at a very young age, to tell the truth. My parents were my models of honesty. If I did something wrong and I told the truth about it, I was punished, but that was the end of it. The punishment always seemed less severe and the consequences far lighter when my misbehavior was rectified by the truth.

My dad always told me, "If you tell the truth, you don't need a very long memory." That's one of the best things about truth: you don't have to waste energy keeping track of what you've told to whom. There's an old saying: "An honest man's pillow is his peace of mind." It's easier to sleep at night when you operate in truth. You don't have to worry about what's going to catch up with you.

That's one of the reasons Jesus emphasized truth. He wants us to have peace of mind, and for leaders, there's perhaps nothing more important. Coaching is hard. We lose. We are criticized in the press. Sometimes we get fired. We deal with many difficulties, and peace of mind is the only variable we can control. I can't control if my teams win or lose, but because of my relationship with Jesus, I can have peace of mind.

The consistent highlighting of truth may not seem to have a huge impact on a daily basis, but eventually a situation will arise in which that commitment is seriously tested, and the capital you have invested over time will pay enormous dividends.

That was the case during the 1999–2000 season, my fifth year as the head coach at Wisconsin. I don't usually enforce a "no drinking" policy, because I want my players to learn how to manage life on their own. But at a Saturday morning practice (on the heels of a 0-3 start in the Big 10), most of the team smelled like a brewery. I lost it.

"As of right now, there will be no drinking the rest of the season," I emphatically stated. "And if you do drink and I find out about it, you'll be suspended for a game!" I made them all sign a piece of paper acknowledging this rule and we moved on.

We ended up having a pretty good year and advanced through the first two rounds of the WNIT. As we prepared for our third-round game, I received an email from a man who was a season ticket holder. He was disappointed because he saw seven of my players out drinking at a bar. I didn't want that email, but I had to deal with it. I didn't have a choice.

I called the team in before practice and told them what I had heard. I asked the seven players to confess, and immediately they all raised their hands. They told me the truth, and I suspended them, just like I had said I would. It was a huge front-page story. Those seven players, including two that were starters, sat out the next game.

Even though we only had seven players in uniform, we still managed to beat Michigan State, 77-45, and the emotionally charged incident carried us all the way to the WNIT title. The suspended players came back to the team after one game on the bench. They told the truth, got a consequence and survived. They knew I valued truth.

All of the players that I suspended became very angry with me. There was one in particular who barely spoke to me during our championship run and the following two months. Then one day she walked into the office and said, "I want to be a part of the solution, not part of the problem." Several years later, I was in her wedding. Dealing with truth had not destroyed her or our relationship.

That's what truth will do. Once you are willing to accept it, the truth will radically change your life. Just ask the Samaritan woman who encountered Jesus at the well in John 4:1-26. When He asked her to bring her husband to Him, she replied, "I don't have a husband" (verse 17). She wasn't telling a lie, but she wasn't telling the truth either. Jesus knew it: "You have correctly said 'I don't have a husband,'" Jesus said. "For you've had five husbands, and the man you now have is not your husband. What you have said is true" (verses 17-18).

Jesus called the woman out, but He did so in love. He accepted her for who she was, but at the same time challenged her to make a change. Jesus values truth. He was the ultimate purveyor of truth. In fact, Jesus was and is still the truth (see John 14:6).

My job as a coach is to confront my players with reality, and that reality must be based in truth. The greatest gift I can give my players is to teach them the value of truth. But if I'm going to teach truth, I have to be above reproach. I can't say that I value truth and then not be truthful myself.

Then, like Jesus, I must dispense that truth with unconditional love that will disarm those under my care. I want to help them understand that truth always wins. As it says in Proverbs 12:19: "Truthful lips endure forever, but a lying tongue, only a moment."

TRAINING TIME

1. In what areas of your life do you struggle with truth?
2. How do you deal with untruthfulness from those you're leading?
3. What are some ways you can begin to create an environment that fosters reciprocal truth among your team or group?

PRAYER

Father, search my heart and shine a spotlight on any untruthfulness that is hidden there. Give me the grace to rid myself

of any dishonest motives and fill me with Your unconditional love.
Help me model truth to those in my care so that they might
lead a life of greater integrity.

Jane Albright is the head women's basketball coach at the University of Nevada. She has coached four different teams to a combined nine NCAA Tournaments and four WNIT bids, including the 2000 championship at Wisconsin. Albright is a four-time conference Coach of the Year and two-time District IV Coach of the Year. She is still the all-time wins leader at both Wisconsin and Northern Illinois.

Find a Mentor, Be a Mentor

PAT WILLIAMS
Senior Vice President, Orlando Magic

*Leading is a two-way street between those at the top
and those trying to get there.*

As I look back on my leadership roles in professional sports, it's crystal clear to me that I never would have made it—never would have had the opportunities I've had—without mentors in my life.

One of my earliest mentors was a man named Bob Carpenter. He was the owner of the Philadelphia Phillies and father of my best friend, Ruly. Following my four years of varsity baseball at Wake Forest, Mr. Carpenter gave me a contract and a $500 bonus to play for his Florida State League farm club in Miami. His last words to me were, "Keep your eyes and ears open on and off the field." That's all he said.

I didn't know then that the scouting report that had come back on me from North Carolina was: "Pretty good catcher. Give him a chance. His real future is in the front office." Once I learned about it, that recommendation had a profound effect on me as I played those two years, because I knew in the back of my mind that they saw something in me that resembled leadership potential.

After my playing days in Florida, the Phillies gave me an opportunity to run minor league teams in their farm system for the next five years. In 1965, I headed to Spartanburg, South Carolina, which was the home of a lower level farm club. That's where a key figure came into my life. His name was R.E. Littlejohn, and he was one of the owners of the Spartanburg team. My dad had been killed in an automobile accident three years prior to that, so Mr. Littlejohn became my surrogate father and my leadership mentor.

In the four years I was with him in Spartanburg, Mr. Littlejohn poured himself into me by spending countless hours with me in his home and office. He was not formally educated, but he loved to teach and counsel. He had a wonderful quality called wisdom. He just delighted in pouring that into me.

Long after I left Spartanburg and transitioned deeply into my NBA career, Mr. Littlejohn was always there for me. I sought him out often and never made a key decision without his counsel and mentoring. He saved me from many falls because he had been down the road and knew where the potholes in life were. To have that wisdom planted in me for so many years was a huge advantage in my future career.

Another mentor who impacted me deeply was Bill Veeck, the great baseball promoter and Hall of Fame executive. Bill took an interest in me during my minor league baseball days and shared his wonderful creativity and imagination freely with me. He was always available by phone, helping me design promotional nights and coming up with creative ways to put people in the ballpark and entertain them once they got there. He was always only a phone call away.

Indeed, aspiring leaders, as I once was, need to seek out mentors, but I've also learned that those who are in leadership have a responsibility to pass wisdom on to the younger generation of budding leaders. That has been one of my greatest joys in life.

I relish the opportunity to play the role of mentor for my children, for people who work for the Orlando Magic, and for people around the country—many of whom I've never formally met.

I feel an enormous obligation to invest back into the next generation. Because of the great experiences I've had and all the generous people who have passed through my life, I have a definite duty to pass that on. There's nothing more fulfilling or more satisfying than to have young people come back and say, "You made a difference. Your counsel was invaluable. I wouldn't be where I am today without your help." It's a joyful experience when you truly impact young people and get them headed in the right direction as leaders.

As a mentor, you don't really know what is getting through to those you are mentoring. You don't realize the impact you're having, but my message to coaches, teachers, youth pastors and anyone who is involved with young people is this: You are not in the coaching business. You are not in the teaching business. You are not in the pastoring business. You really are in the leadership development business. That's what you're doing full-time. When you recognize this, it will change the way you coach, teach and lead. Your job is to pour into the youth and do everything you can to get them ready to lead in the future—in their homes, in their communities, in their churches and on their sports teams. That's your assignment.

In 2006, my son Bobby was managing a club in Savannah, Georgia, part of the Washington Nationals farm system. It's about a four-hour drive from Orlando, and I would go up there a few weekends during the season. There was a young girl in her early 20s, Katie Stocz, who was just out of college and helping run the front office. She was all over that ballpark, doing the water balloons, overseeing the dizzy bat contest, going up in the stands greeting special groups, and getting on the microphone between innings. She was a spitfire.

Over time, Katie made a deep impression on me. Later that fall, my assistant left and I asked Katie if she might be interested in working for me. She turned me down, saying she wanted to stay with baseball. About a month later, she called back, said she had changed her mind, and asked if we could revisit our discussion. I had already filled the post, but I invited her down for an interview with our front office. They hired her on the spot. She's now in her fifth year with us and she's a star. Our paths cross in the office every other week or so, and she always gives me a hug and thanks me for helping open the door. I tell her, "Katie, you're making me look real good."

Her response: "And I always will."

For those out there like Katie, looking to advance into a leadership position, here are some guidelines for how you should pursue a relationship with a mentor:

1. **Seek out mentors.** Ask them to be of help to you. Don't be bashful. Many young people think, "I don't want to bother them. They wouldn't have time. I don't want to be a pest." It's amazing to me, particularly as people with years of experience get older and go into retirement, how people forget them. So to young people, you would be shocked by what delight older people get out of being asked to be a mentor. Do not hesitate to ask.

2. **Find mentors in different areas.** You might need a mentor in the business area of your life. You might need a mentor in the spiritual area. You might need another mentor in the area of marriage or family relations. There's nothing wrong with having a multitude of mentors with specialties in different areas of life.

3. **Follow the mentor's advice.** When the mentor counsels and advises, I strongly recommend following it. Nothing discourages mentors faster than when they pour themselves into you and give you every bit of their wisdom, and then you do the opposite of what they have suggested. If that happens too often, that mentor is going to be an ex-mentor. If you're seeking wisdom from them and they give you counsel, I urge you to follow their advice.

Likewise, here are some things that will be helpful to potential leadership mentors looking for ways to share their experience with the younger generation:

1. **You are the pursued, not the pursuer.** The burden is on the younger person. Mr. Littlejohn, Bill Veeck, Bob Carpenter—they weren't chasing me down trying to say, "It's time for a mentoring session." I was always chasing them down when things came up and I needed counseling, insight and wisdom.

2. **The mentoring relationship does not have to be on a formal basis.** It can be a formal meeting such as, "Every Tuesday morning we're meeting for breakfast," but it can also be very informal. It doesn't even have to be in person. Most of my mentoring with Mr. Littlejohn, particularly after I left Spartanburg, was by phone. I didn't see a lot of Mr. Littlejohn, but I probably talked to him on the phone a couple of times a week. It doesn't have to be formal and regimented by a schedule.

3. **Don't be resentful of other mentors.** There can be a sense of possessiveness or ownership that says, "I'm mentoring that young person and I don't want anyone

else in his or her life." Don't be clingy, fragile or resentful if the person you are mentoring also seeks counsel from other people. Don't cause that individual to become nervous and be forced to mask their emotions because they sense you might be upset that there are other mentors in their lives.

As you study the Bible carefully, you'll find many examples of outstanding leaders who understood the importance of mentoring. King Solomon sat down and penned the Proverbs, which really are just written forms of mentoring. Long before Zig Ziglar, Tony Robbins or Brian Tracy came along, Solomon provided all the material that those of us who are motivational speakers would ever need. So much of what we speak about is from the Proverbs, dressed up in a twenty-first-century covering. Solomon wrote all of it for us. He was a mentor long before there was probably a word for it.

"Without guidance, people fall," Solomon wrote in Proverbs 11:14, "but with many counselors there is deliverance." The apostle Paul also did a lot of mentoring. He loved to have young people around him, and he poured his life into them. Paul famously mentored Timothy, Titus and Philemon through the exhortative letters that we have access to in the New Testament. The rest of Paul's writings—to the churches in Rome, Corinth, Galatia, Ephesus, Philippi, Colossae and Thessalonica—were essentially group mentoring sessions that have been passed down for more than 2,000 years.

But there has never been a greater mentor than Jesus. He had 12 disciples around Him, and He spent most of the time mentoring them. He poured Himself into their lives. He instructed them and taught them and advised them. He steered them and prepared them for the time when they would be without His physical presence on earth.

We read throughout the Gospels about the many times Jesus taught the masses through a parable and then pulled the disciples aside and gave them even deeper insight into the timeless truth He had just spoken. What a gift these men were given, to be able to spend time with the One who was so often addressed as "Rabbi," or "Teacher."

Principled leadership in our society will not continue without the wisdom and experience that is passed down from generation to generation through the act of mentoring. As young people, you don't have time in life to make 15,000 mistakes that could have been avoided. You'll be 80 years old and still picking yourself up off the ground. A wise young person has mentors in his or her life. So, to all aspiring leaders, find a godly mentor and allow him or her to help direct your path.

For our leaders out there, you must realize how important it is that you become a mentor. The impact that you have as coaches is second to none. We live in a sports-crazy nation. Coaches have a level of influence that's unimaginable. The words you say, the actions you take and the way you express yourself leave a deep imprint on every athlete that crosses your path.

Because of what's taking place in this nation in this generation, your role as a coach has taken on far more significance than ever before. Mentoring has never been at a higher premium. So, to all the experienced leaders, be available to the young people around you and help them build a bridge to a more successful and productive future.

TRAINING TIME

1. Who is someone you would consider to be one of your past or present mentors, and how has that person impacted your life as a leader?

2. If you have someone whom you mentor on a regular basis, how has that interaction made a difference in his or her life? How has it blessed you?
3. To aspiring leaders: How can you start the process of seeking a mentor today? To aspiring mentors: How can you make yourself available to the young people within your sphere of influence?

PRAYER

Father, give me a heart for mentoring. If I need to be mentored by a wiser, more experienced leader, direct my path to that person's doorstep. If I need to be a mentor to others, give me the patience, discipline and wisdom to pour into the lives of those who seek my counsel.

Pat Williams is the senior vice president of the NBA's Orlando Magic. As general manager of the Philadelphia 76ers, he helped build the 1983 NBA championship team that featured Hall of Fame inductees Julius Erving and Moses Malone. Williams is also a popular motivational speaker and author of more than 70 books, including *The Warrior Within*, *What Are You Living For*, *The Pursuit* and his latest title, *Extreme Focus*.

Seek Wise Counsel

STEVE FITZHUGH

Executive Director of PowerMoves and Retired NFL Player

Leading isn't a one-person job.

One of the best pieces of advice I ever received came from Oscar Roan, a retired tight end who had played for the Cleveland Browns. It was the summer before my freshman year at Miami University of Ohio, and Roan was giving his testimony at my church.

After the program, I stuck my chest out, threw my shoulders back and carried my 173 pounds up to the front to ask a question: "Mr. Roan, I've got a full scholarship to Miami University of Ohio. Can you give me some advice? I'd like to play in the NFL one day."

What he told me shaped my college career and changed my future. He said, "Son, the first thing you do when you get to college is find the people who know how to pray and build relationships with them."

That wasn't what I was expecting him to say, but still, I took his advice. When I got to college, I hooked up with the Navigators ministry (there wasn't an FCA group on campus at the time). I built relationships with those guys, and they were my spiritual teammates. At the time, I had never heard the word "accountability," but since then I've learned the true value of that principle as a leader and as a follower of Christ.

Accountability is the practice of regularly subjecting one's motives and actions to a responsible partner or partners for the purpose of receiving guidance and correction for healthy and proper life direction. Without this principle, the subtle seduction of errant thinking can be accepted as a "best practice," and can skew perspective and contaminate leadership decisions.

Until my college career, I had been on my own spiritually. I grew up in a family that didn't go to church. I was surrounded by the influence of drugs, alcohol and abuse. I overcame a lot of that, yet the real key for me was when, at 12 years old, I met Jesus Christ. That was the first time I found out there was a plan—and I was part of it. My encounter with Christ changed everything because somewhere deep in my mind I knew that life as I was experiencing it wasn't the way it was supposed to be.

Over time, my leadership role in college blossomed. Many of the African-American players on the team weren't plugged into a Bible study, so I invited them to go with me. Eventually, I felt led to start a separate Bible study for my teammates. On Saturday nights, when everyone else was out partying and doing all kinds of crazy stuff, we would get a six-pack of cream soda and head back to the dormitory to watch the Trinity Broadcasting Network (TBN).

After my playing career ended, I moved to Washington, DC, and began working with FCA. That's when I really started to understand the biblical context for this concept of accountability. My immediate supervisor was Dan Britton, then the Northern Virginia area director. He introduced me to a place called Starbucks and a drink called the caramel macchiato, and every Thursday we would sit, pray and talk for an hour in my downtown DC office.

During this time, I quickly came to understand the priceless benefits of accountability. I experienced firsthand the truth found in Proverbs 15:22, where Solomon writes, "Plans fail when there is no counsel, but with many advisers they succeed." If the wisest man who has ever lived insists that wise counsel is paramount to success, then I firmly believe that accountability is going to produce strong and lasting benefits. Success, safety and wisdom are all available to those who humbly submit to healthy voices of counsel in their lives.

I've also seen what happens to leaders who ignore this principle and get too comfortable leaning on their own understanding. Predicating all of your decision-making on one isolated perspective is a very dangerous thing to do. It's in isolation that our insulation against thoughts and conclusions that are not true north breaks down. Unchecked, we can unknowingly head down the wrong path, at the wrong time, with the wrong information. When a leader does this, it can be catastrophic.

In order to achieve biblical accountability, leaders must seek out three things: right fellowship (see Colossians 3:12-14), right advisors (see Proverbs 15:22), and godly training with the right people (see 1 Timothy 4:7-10). For me, that means I am in daily contact with one or two men who hear my revelations, challenges, hopes, dreams, goals and insights. We encourage one another, inspire one another and rebuke one another when necessary.

It's important to remember that accountability is a two-way street. Sometimes you might get called out for heading down the wrong path. Sometimes it might be your job to let your brother or sister in Christ know that he or she is headed for danger. Jesus displayed this principle in the way He led by relationship. He held the 12 disciples accountable through His words, His teachings and His actions.

Sometimes, Christ's methods of accountability weren't pleasant. Take for example His exchange with Peter in Matthew 16:21-23:

> From then on Jesus began to point out to His disciples
> that He must go to Jerusalem and suffer many things

from the elders, chief priests, and scribes, be killed, and be raised the third day. Then Peter took Him aside and began to rebuke Him, "Oh no, Lord! This will never happen to you!" But He turned and told Peter, "Get behind Me, Satan! You are an offense to Me because you're not thinking about God's concerns, but man's."

I doubt Peter enjoyed being rebuked like that, but later on he would become the cornerstone for the Church. And because of Christ's leadership and attention to accountability, the Church lives today. That's why accountability is so vital to us as Christian leaders. God wants to see our potential fulfilled. He wants us to do great things in His name. As it says in Proverbs 27:17, "Iron sharpens iron, and one man sharpens another." Leadership is not a one-person job. We need each other to make the most of the individual gifts and abilities God has bestowed upon us.

TRAINING TIME

1. What kind of spiritual accountability do you have set up in your life?
2. Can you tell the difference between times when you've stayed true to that accountability and times when you've strayed from it?
3. What are some ways you can strengthen your relationships with other likeminded leaders, both as an exhorter and as a disciple within the accountability partnership?

PRAYER

Father, give me the courage to reach out to trustworthy people who can help me stay accountable to my commitment to You.

Place the right people in my path and lay down a foundation for a long and healthy partnership that benefits the spiritual, emotional and physical well-being of all involved.

Steve Fitzhugh is the executive director of PowerMoves and founder of The House, a youth center in Washington, DC. Fitzhugh was an All-Conference football player at Miami University of Ohio and spent two years in the NFL playing for the Denver Broncos. He has authored four books and speaks nationally as the spokesperson for FCA's One Way 2 Play: Drug Free program.

Encouragement Builds Others Up

BRUCE MATTHEWS

NFL Hall of Fame Offensive Lineman

Leading a team to success requires positive reinforcement.

In 19 years as an NFL player, I can't say I truly understood the power of encouragement until I had experienced the destructive nature of its counterpart: discouragement. I'm certain that's why the coaches that struck a chord with me were the ones who encouraged me to be the best player possible.

There was no greater example of encouragement to me than Les Steckel. For five years, he was my offensive coordinator, including the 1999 season when the Titans went to the Super Bowl. Without fail, Coach Steckel would encourage the team with a halftime speech or a Monday morning talk before looking at the game film. Even if we were stinking it up on the field, it was comforting to know that he hadn't given up on us. Coach Steckel honestly believed that we were going to find a way to work it out.

It was only after he left the Titans that I realized what a special gift he had been giving us. When encouragement is there, you might take it for granted, but once it's gone, you're very aware of the void. Later, as a coach, I looked into my past for insight into how to relate to my players. Many of the principles and attitudes I want to portray come from my memories of how Coach Steckel used to do it.

Unfortunately, encouraging words are often few and far between at all levels of coaching. It's a cliché sometimes, but the player is usually his own worst critic. When a player makes a mistake, he knows before anyone else. We joke about it a lot, but coaches often point out the obvious to their players. Instead of reliving their mistakes, players want to know how to fix the problem.

That's the problem with criticism. When that's all the players hear, they stop listening, and whatever the coach is trying to accomplish is rendered powerless. Negativity is the easiest thing to fall back on. As coaches and leaders, you have to be mindful of your attitude and avoid the temptation to be negative.

Instead, always look for the higher ground and emphasize the positives. It's important to have other believers around you to keep you accountable in this area. I've told my assistant offensive line coach, Art Valero, to let me know if I get negative or if my coaching ever becomes about me. I want him to call me out. I know how bad it felt when I was a player and coaches used those tactics on me.

We are not naturally inclined to be encouragers. Early on in our faith, doing what the Holy Spirit wants us to do is radically different from what seems natural to our flesh. It seems like stepping off a precipice, thinking we're going to take a dive. But as we exercise that faith muscle more and more, it becomes easier and God entrusts us with more.

The apostles and the Early Church provide an incredible example of encouragement. Paul's letters were an encouragement to younger Christians like Timothy and Titus. The Church had a singleness of purpose and persevered despite so much martyrdom. Living for Christ took priority over everything in their lives, including their personal well-being. The only way they could survive was by relying on one another's encouraging words.

Those early Christians were really just following Jesus' example. Every word Jesus spoke was for our encouragement. There has never been a greater model of this principle. Jesus always encouraged His disciples and the people whom He encountered. In Matthew 14:27, the disciples were in a boat and saw someone walking on the lake. It was Jesus, and He said to them, "Have courage! It is I. Don't be afraid."

When Jesus spoke to His disciples about how He would be betrayed and killed, they were afraid of what was going to happen when He was gone. He told them in John 14:1, "Your heart must not be troubled." Later on in that chapter, Jesus encouraged them by revealing that the Holy Spirit would soon come to "teach you all things and remind you of everything I have told you" (verse 26).

Jesus could have been angered by the disciples' fear and doubt. He could have scolded them for their unbelief and lack of faith. Instead, He encouraged them and gave them helpful instructions that would eventually help them plant the seeds for one of the greatest revivals in history.

As a coach, and as a person, that's the model I want to follow. I want to encourage and equip my players, my children, my wife and anyone else within my circle of influence to be the best at what God has called them to be.

TRAINING TIME

1. Do you find it easy or difficult to be encouraging in the face of discouraging circumstances?

2. How have you seen encouragement improve a bad situation?
3. Which attributes of Christ do you think might help you have a more encouraging and positive spirit while leading others?

PRAYER

Father, give me the wisdom to only use words of encouragement in order to build up those whom I am leading. Give me the grace to resist the temptation to be negative and use discouraging words that might tear others down.

Bruce Matthews is a 19-year NFL veteran, 14-time Pro Bowl selection and member of the Pro Football Hall of Fame. He spent his entire playing career within the Oilers/Titans organization and was a key member of Tennessee's 1999–2000 AFC Championship team. Matthews is currently serving as the Titans' offensive line coach.

Run for the Prize

LANCE BERKMAN
MLB Outfielder

Leading to win yields the ultimate victory.

Christians don't care about winning.

That's one of the biggest knocks on Christian competitors. It's also one of the biggest myths.

People who assume that Christians have a lackadaisical competitive spirit don't have a good working knowledge of the God of the Bible. All you have to do is read some of the Old Testament stories and some key passages in the New Testament. God doesn't fool around, and He expects His followers to be as zealous as He is. The Bible makes it clear that whatever we do, we should do it as unto the Lord (see Colossians 3:17). That simply means we should do it to our fullest ability.

Consider this story, found in Numbers 25: Phinehas, grandson of Aaron the priest, drives a spear through a rebellious Israelite man and an idolatrous Midianite woman and pins them to the ground. The Lord rewarded him for his zealousness. There are many examples in the Old Testament of God telling the people of Israel to defeat their enemies and wipe them out.

We live in a different time. We are no longer on the battle-field literally fighting God's enemies. Instead, we are to strive for excellence and make an effort to be the best at whatever we've been called to do. Our charge is the same, whether on the play-ing field, in ministry, in community service, in the corporate world or any other place God may have placed us.

Our desire for excellence must be based not on our emotions but rather on our understanding of who God is and what He re-quires of us. Baseball is a game of many failures. Good hitters are successful only one-third of the time. Thirty teams compete each year for one championship. Based on my emotions alone, there are times when I can't stand this sport.

It can be the same way in our Christian walks. There may be times when we're sorely tempted to abandon our principles, and that's when it comes down to an act of will. It's something we train ourselves to do. It's part of the sanctification process—learning how to apply our wills and how to push on during those times when we don't feel like it. It's not an emotional roller coaster. It's steadier and it's much deeper.

It's a lot like being married. I've been married for over ten years now. This is rare, but every once in a while my wife and I are at odds with each other, and we don't necessarily feel loving to-wards each other. But the love we have for each other is a lot deeper than that. It's not born of emotion; it comes from our wills. Your Christian walk has to be the same way. Your desire to please God and push for excellence is an act of will.

This is especially true for those of us who are in positions of leadership. When we set an example that portrays a strong em-phasis on excellence, those who are following us will want to know more about the God we serve. You can never overstate the importance of using your platform or the position you've been given to effect good in every circumstance. The only reason I'm in the position I'm in is that God has gifted me and has seen fit to put me here. I have to honor that by using my influence and my status on the team and in the game of baseball for good and to bring about His purpose.

Personally, I don't struggle to reconcile my competitive nature with my spiritual act of service to God. In fact, I believe they can be one and the same. In 1 Corinthians 9:24, the apostle Paul writes, "Do you not know that the runners in a stadium all race, but only one receives the prize? Run in such a way that you may win."

When I'm out there, I'm out there to win. I know that I'm not going to win every game. I know that my team won't win the championship every season. Still, I give my best, knowing that excellence and the pursuit of a victorious life are what God wants from me.

Later in the same passage, Paul reveals this important truth: "Therefore I do not run like one who runs aimlessly, or box like one who beats the air. Instead, I discipline my body and bring it under strict control, so that after preaching to others, I myself will not be disqualified" (1 Corinthians 9:26-27).

Some Christians have done a disservice to the faith by backing off from competitive excellence. People respect determination. They respect desire. They respect people who want to be good and excellent in all areas of their lives. If you claim to be a Christian, and yet you're not working as hard as you could, or you're not giving a full effort or competing to win, people aren't going to take you seriously in other areas. I've always believed that Christians should work harder than anybody else.

Take an athlete like Tim Tebow, for example. Look at the platform he's obtained because of the way he plays. People respect him tremendously for the way he carries himself on the field, the way he competes to win, and the way he demands the same from his teammates. He is a prime example of a Christian who is doing it the right way. Tim Tebow is going to have a bigger impact than somebody who is negligent in the area of competitive excellence.

Does this mean that I pray for a hit or ask God to help me win? No, because I want to do the best that I can do and let whatever happens, happen. There's an element of chance in life that you can't account for, and you have to understand that there are more important things than the outcome of any given contest or confrontation.

As Paul writes in 1 Corinthians 9:25, "Now everyone who competes exercises self-control in everything. However, they do it to receive a perishable crown, but we an imperishable one." In other words, as Christians we are playing or working or striving for excellence because we know there's something wonderful waiting for us—something even better than an MVP title, an All-Star Game or a World Series ring.

Jesus exemplified this commitment to competitive excellence in His life on earth. He didn't leave His celestial home and take the form of a man just to do His best and see how things might play out. He came to win. He came to be victorious. He came to defeat Satan and take back the keys of death and hell so that those who believe in Him might live forever in heaven. As we read in the book of Revelation, Jesus will come again one day and defeat our enemy once and for all.

In the meantime, what better way to honor Him than to give our absolute best in every area of our lives and walk in the victory He has already won?

TRAINING TIME

1. Do you find it easy or difficult to balance your competitive nature with your desire to be like Christ? Explain.
2. How does 1 Corinthians 9:24-27 speak to you personally about your competitive life and your position as a Christian leader?

3. What are some ways that you can use both your competitive successes and failures to bring glory to God and win others to Christ?

PRAYER

Father, give me a zeal to pursue excellence every day and in every aspect of my life. Help me to fully understand that competition is merely a vehicle by which I might bring glory to Your name and expand Your kingdom.

Lance Berkman is an outfielder with the St. Louis Cardinals. He previously spent the bulk of his career as the first baseman for the Houston Astros, leading that club to its first World Series appearance in 2005. Berkman, who has also played for the New York Yankees, is a five-time National League All-Star selection.

Serve as an Example

MADELINE MANNING-MIMS
Olympic Gold Medalist, Track and Field

Leading as a servant inspires others to serve.

Servanthood is an act of worship that fulfills the Great Commission (see Matthew 28:18-20). It reveals the heart of God, which is His love for all people. A servant leader's heart puts love into action and leads by example. It's easy to tell those following you that they should serve, but it's hard to lead others where you have not been.

My mother, Queen, was a model of servant leadership in our inner-city home in Cleveland, Ohio. She served as a lay minister to the sick, the shut-in and the bereaved. I always tagged along with her when I was young. There was something about her spirit of compassion that captured my interest.

Mother seemed to frequent funeral homes, comforting those who had lost loved ones and signing each family's guest book. I remember going around viewing the different bodies and signing the guest books. I noticed that many had only a small number of guests to sign in. Looking back, I suppose the funeral director may have wondered how I knew all these deceased people!

I was never afraid of the dead because in my little mind, it was a time when they were all spiffed up in their nice clothes with their hair nicely done. They were just sleeping while people came to see them and lovingly weep over their departure to heaven to be with Jesus. Then, it was time to sign the book and go eat like pigs! My love for the bereaved and the sick grew in my heart from these trips with my mom.

The joy of serving others continued to take root. When I was about 9 or 10 years old, I often took care of the other neighborhood children during my playtime. I would organize games in the projects where I lived, giving the mothers a needed break. I also shared my family's food with those who were hungry. I was unaware of the miracle of multiplication God was performing in our home. The supernatural was a natural phenomenon for me. I later came to understand that it's impossible to serve without God's help.

As I became a competitive runner, the desire to serve others continued. I had a knack for helping other runners reach their goals by running at their pace. I always encouraged them before and after each race. Sometimes I would pray with them before a big meet, like the U.S. Olympic Trials. I often made myself available to my competitors and teammates to listen and give godly counsel.

Sometimes it kept me up, or woke me up, late at night when someone was experiencing crisis. In 1980, I was in Rome with the U.S. Track Team and was the women's captain. The night before my race in the 800 meters, I was up until four in the morning with a distraught teammate who had awakened me at 1:30 to talk, cry and pray. My husband, who was there along with my son, got a firsthand view of what my life on the team was really like.

The next day, I ran an embarrassing, lethargic race because I lacked the rest my body needed to compete at a world-class level. Nevertheless, I answered the call to serve and have no regrets about doing so.

That call has only intensified throughout my life. While training for my Master of Divinity degree at Oral Roberts University, I served as a hospital chaplain at the Hillcrest Medical Center in Tulsa, Oklahoma. I became known as "the singing chaplain." When I prayed for some of the patients, oftentimes I would also sing to them. The music seemed to soothe their souls with the peace, comfort and presence of Jesus. I only did this at the prompting of the Holy Spirit.

One time I was visiting an elderly man with gloriously white hair. We talked, I prayed, and then I asked him if I could sing something for him. He looked at me with a surprised look on his face, smiled and said, "Sure, go right ahead." I was puzzled when "America, the Beautiful" came into my mind. But without question I began to sing. He started to weep, and then joined in the song with his magnificent baritone voice. The nurses and doctor stopped at the door to listen, and when we finished singing, they gave us an ovation. The patient then told me that he was a decorated veteran from the Korean War, and how that song meant more to him than I knew.

Unfortunately, many people today have an attitude of entitlement, always looking to receive something and not being willing to give. If only we could all understand the sense of worth, joy and fulfillment that serving others brings. Serving also builds good character, and while a true servant is not looking for rewards, they are overjoyed when the blessings come.

Servant leadership is not easy. It opposes our human nature. That's why it's so important to have daily fellowship with our heavenly Father in prayer and the Word. It's also helpful to journal. The next step I take is to ask the Holy Spirit to lead and guide me in fulfilling the Father's will. During the day, I try to remain sensitive to the Holy Spirit's leading in meeting my earthly assignments by looking for those opportunities where He wants me to serve.

There are so many ways to serve others. Look for opportunities to serve in the small things. A word of encouragement or praise can change someone's day. Notice people's accomplishments or positive progress and acknowledge them. Look for areas of need where you may have something to give. Lend a helping hand when you can, and always be ready to pray with people in times of joy and sorrow. Use your talents and gifts to be a blessing to others.

Above all, study and follow Christ's example of servant leadership. He came to serve humanity by doing the Father's will. If the King of glory could humble Himself and become a servant, how much more ought I to do the same and fulfill the Father's will in my life? I owe Him everything, and I will serve Him because He first served me. I am humbled by His grace and mercy over my life. I am thankful for my salvation through Jesus Christ my Lord.

Jesus is the greatest leader ever, and He proved it on Calvary by serving all humanity with the gift of eternal life. He did so in order to show us the heart of the Father, a heart of love. Servanthood cost Jesus His life. We too must die to ourselves and live lives of servanthood to the glory of Jesus, the ultimate servant.

TRAINING TIME

1. Who are some people you've seen exemplify servant leadership and what about their character do you admire most?
2. What are some benefits you've experienced from serving others?
3. What does following the Holy Spirit's leading look like for you? What is the difference between the times you've followed Him and times you haven't?

PRAYER

Father, fill my heart with Your perfect love and help me follow Your Spirit as I look for opportunities to serve those I lead and others who cross my path.

Madeline Manning-Mims is a four-time Olympian for the U.S. in track. Manning-Mims won the gold medal in the 800-meter race at the 1968 Olympics and the silver medal in the 4 x 400 meter relay at the 1972 Olympics. Manning-Mims also collected an 800-meter gold at the 1967 Pan American Games. She is the founder and president of the United States Council for Sports Chaplaincy and has served as a chaplain at the last six Summer Olympic Games. She is also a WNBA chaplain for the Tulsa Shock.

Stick to the Plan

KYLE KORVER
NBA Shooting Guard

Leading is a disciplined journey along God's path.

In today's world, there are so many distractions and different directions we can go that it's easy to get sidetracked. But when you stick to the plan God has laid out before you, He will take care of the rest and get you where you're going. In order to be effective leaders, we must first know God's plan and then move forward boldly and confidently in that plan.

When I graduated from Creighton, my whole goal was to make the NBA. That was the plan. I went to school, got an education and graduated. I took care of those important things, but the plan was always to go to the NBA. It wasn't until the pre-draft workouts that I had any doubts at all. All of a sudden, my back started bothering me. For the first time, I had fears that maybe this wouldn't happen.

On the morning of my graduation, my dad, Kevin Korver, woke up early. He felt God prompt him to pray Proverbs 3:5-6 over me. While I was still asleep, he got up and spoke these words: "Trust in the LORD with all your heart, and do not rely on your own understanding; think about Him in all your ways, and He will guide you on the right paths." Then he went back to bed.

Later that morning, my mom gave my dad a graduation card to sign. There was a Bible verse printed inside the card at the bottom. It was Proverbs 3:5-6. He immediately knew he needed to tell me about what had happened a few hours earlier. With all that was going on in my life, hearing that meant the world to me.

For the next two months leading up to the NBA draft, I prayed that verse at least 20 times a day—or at least, it seemed like 20 times a day. On draft day, I was barely picked. It was late in the second round when New Jersey chose me—with the fifty-first selection out of 58. I wasn't even selected on live television. It happened during a commercial break. Even worse, or so I thought, I was traded to Philadelphia later that night. Philly was the last place I wanted to play. There wasn't anything wrong with the team or the coach. I just didn't feel comfortable with their style of play, and I wasn't happy about moving to the East Coast.

A month later, my dad was praying for me in his office, which happens to be located in my youngest brother's former bedroom. The room was decorated with sports posters and some of his boys' old trophies and plaques. One particular framed photo caught my dad's attention. It was a picture of me walking off the court on senior night at Creighton. I was pointing toward my family in the crowd. Then my dad noticed something else. The way the picture was positioned, it looked like I was pointing towards the back of my brother's door, and lo and behold, right there was hanging a poster of Allen Iverson playing with the Philadelphia 76ers.

Of course, my dad knew that this was another story he had to share with me. At that point, all I could say was, "All right, God." It wasn't the situation I wanted, but I knew it was where He wanted me to be at that time in my career. So I continued to work hard, and I stuck to the principles I'd lived by to that point. Along with taking care of my spiritual needs, I kept lifting weights, tried

to get plenty of sleep and, as Coach John Wooden might emphasize, laced up my shoes the right way every day.

When discussing Proverbs 3:5-6, most people focus on the
first section of the passage, the charge to trust in God and not
lean on your own understanding. But the best part is what happens when you do those things. You are able to benefit from the
promise that says, "He will guide you on the right paths."

That's exactly what happened in Philadelphia. While playing my first five seasons there, I grew as both a leader and an athlete on the court. In fact, one of my best years was 2006–2007,
when I came off the bench but averaged a career-high 14.4 points
per game. Behind the scenes, I was introduced to FCA chaplain
Kevin Harvey, who led our pre-game Bible studies. His leadership made a big impact on my spiritual growth.

I'd always leaned on God, but I don't think I really grasped
what being a Christian was all about until those first few years
in the NBA. I saw the negative things that getting wrapped up in
basketball can bring. That, more than anything, drew me closer
to God and helped prepare me to be more assertive in my role as
a Christian leader.

It's not always an easy road. We can see that in the life of Christ,
who sacrificed His perfect existence in heaven with the Father in order to walk alongside mankind in a very imperfect world. Because
He knew there was a purpose and a plan for His life as a human, He
could trust that despite the hardship, pain and suffering He would
endure, it would be worth every step of the journey.

Just like in Jesus' story, your decision about whether or not
to follow God's path comes down to whether or not you trust
that He has a plan. It's easy to look at a situation or have a goal
and work out in your mind the exact steps you think you need
to take. But that's not always the path God has in mind for you.
As they say, "When you pray, expect the unexpected." God often
works things out in ways we don't anticipate. But we can always

lean on the truth found in Jeremiah 29:11: " 'For I know the plans I have for you'—[this is] the Lord's declaration—'plans for [your] welfare, not for disaster, to give you a future and a hope.' "

Then you have to ask yourself this question: "Am I 100 percent willing to admit that everything I have is loaned, not owned?" If you are, then you'll be at peace with whatever God has for you at the end of that path.

TRAINING TIME

1. Can you think of a time in your life when God clearly showed you which way to go? Did you follow His leading? How did things turn out?
2. What are some distractions you deal with while trying to pursue God's will for your life as a leader? How have those distractions negatively impacted your ability to lead?
3. When following the path for your life, why is it important to understand that the things you have—your talents, abilities, opportunities, resources, and so on—don't belong to you but have been loaned to you by God?

PRAYER

Father, show me the path upon which You want me to walk, and if I can't see the end from here, help me trust that You will guide me in the right direction and lead me to a destination where my hope, my future and my peace will be found.

Kyle Korver is a shooting guard who plays for the NBA's Chicago Bulls. At Creighton University, he set a Missouri Valley Conference record with 371 career three-pointers and was twice named MVC Player of the Year. Korver also became Creighton's first player to appear in four consecutive NCAA Tournaments.

Good Things Take Time

JERRY KINDALL

Retired Head Baseball Coach, University of Arizona

Leading is an exercise in patience.

As a coach, you learn pretty quickly how much patience you have, or most likely, don't have. Baseball is especially trying on one's patience. As a player, you deal with batting slumps, or it might be an issue of waiting for good pitches at the plate. As a coach, it can be frustrating when players don't respond to your teaching. A losing streak can be the downfall of an entire team's patience.

For nearly 60 years, I've been around the game of baseball as a player, a coach, a consultant, a chaplain and a broadcaster. After my eight-year Major League career, I was given the opportunity to become an assistant coach with the University of Minnesota baseball team. Then, in 1972, I took the job at Arizona, where I coached for 25 years. I felt like I belonged in the college game. I even turned down an offer to manage in the Major Leagues. I know the Lord placed me in college baseball for a reason, and I'm convinced it was partly so He could teach me patience.

It took me a long time to learn this principle, because I'm an impatient guy. I was always looking for perfection. I never found it in my own life, so I expected it out of my players. Over time, I gradually learned how to be patient through the grace of the Holy Spirit. Understanding the value of patience helped to calm me down as a coach. I began to see my players and assistant coaches in the light of God's creation, and I recognized how He had brought them into my life. Patience helped me to understand them more, reach out to them more, and be more tolerant and gracious with them. They were just college kids, after all.

I also stopped looking at myself as their ultimate authority; instead, I started regarding myself as a servant to them. In God's scheme of things, I'm called to be a servant and to reflect God's mercy and grace in Christ Jesus. I knew that all along, but I just couldn't overcome my own selfishness and ego early in my career. Eventually I came to understand that good things take time. Often that means patiently waiting for God's plan to be fulfilled.

God's Word has been my source of inspiration and challenge when it comes to exercising patience. One of my favorite passages of Scripture is Ephesians 4:1-3, in which the apostle Paul exhorts us: "Live a life worthy of the calling you have received. Be completely humble and gentle; be patient, bearing with one another in love. Make every effort to keep the unity of the Spirit through the bond of peace" (*NIV*).

When I read that passage, I'm immediately reminded of how Jesus led His disciples. He patiently taught them His ways and lovingly allowed for their growing pains and immature mistakes. Even when He rebuked them, He did so with a spirit of humility and gentleness to preserve unity within the group. Most importantly, Jesus never gave up on them.

There is no better example of patient leadership than Jesus Christ. We have a clear record of the impact Jesus had on those who followed Him. They were the ones who founded the Early

Church and turned the world upside down by spreading the message of the gospel. We, as leaders today, can have the same impact on those under our watch. As we exercise unyielding patience, we can reap the blessing of seeing them go on to even greater things for God's glory.

TRAINING TIME

1. As a leader, what are some things that test your patience?
2. In what ways have you seen impatience negatively impact your leadership effectiveness?
3. What are some steps you can take that will help you to become a more patient leader?

PRAYER

Father, grant me patience every morning as I prepare for my day. Teach me how to use the same kind of humility, gentleness and kindness as Jesus exercised in leading His disciples.

Jerry Kindall is the former head baseball coach at the University of Arizona, where he led the Wildcats to three College World Series titles in a 25-year span. Kindall also spent eight years in the Major Leagues, playing with the Chicago Cubs, the Cleveland Indians and the Minnesota Twins, for whom he played in the 1965 World Series. He has worked extensively with USA Baseball and stays close to the game as a spring training chaplain and part-time consultant.

Actions Speak Louder than Words

CLARK KELLOGG

Lead College Basketball Analyst, CBS Sports

Leading is more walk and less talk.

To be effective as a leader, you've got to walk your talk. Leadership in its broadest context is role modeling and mentoring. In other words, the walk is all about setting an example for others, because "actions speak louder than words."

I've been around leaders that set a great example based on Christlike principles, but I didn't usually appreciate it until I was far removed from the situation. Certainly much of my understanding of this principle came through my sports experience, but it first started in my home.

My dad was a policeman in Cleveland for over 40 years, and he worked additional part-time jobs to support his five children. He set a noteworthy example for us with his consistent hard work and provision. I also saw how my parents treated folks when they came to our home. It was kind of a gathering place for many of our family members and friends. A lot of that had to do with how welcoming my parents were. They set an example by treating people the way they would want to be treated.

Another great example for me was Clayton Burroughs, my sixth-grade teacher. He was one of the few male teachers I had throughout elementary and middle school. Mr. Burroughs was also one of the few African-American teachers at the time. He was firm and demanding, but consistent. Students and fellow faculty members greatly respected him. His example laid the foundation for what I could aspire to be.

When you lead in a way that sets a godly example, you become a respected resource for other people. You end up being a positive influencer when you present a consistent example. You become someone that people will look to for inspiration, counsel or advice.

I have tremendous respect for Tony Dungy and the example he set in his position as a head coach. He has impacted thousands of people through his example, consistency and authenticity. It's because of his attributes and the platform God has given him that he has been able to be a great example for so many. People who are examples in leadership become influencers on a wide scale.

When you understand the value of setting that example, you hold yourself to a higher standard. When there's a level of expectation of you as a leader, you automatically have an anchor of accountability, first to God and then to those people who are following (and watching) you.

When I consider my responsibility as a leader and the example I want to set each day, I must first make sure that I am consistently in intimate fellowship with the Lord through time spent in prayer and meditation on the Word of God. I need to spend time in the Father's presence. That helps me align myself with Him and see things with a biblical perspective. If I'm moving to be more like Him, I'm on track to become the example God wants me to be.

There's a hallmark passage that helps me understand what it means to be that Christlike example. It's 2 Peter 1:5-8:

> Make every effort to supplement your faith with goodness, goodness with knowledge, knowledge with self-control, self-control with endurance, endurance with godliness, godliness with brotherly affection, and brotherly affection with love. For if these qualities are yours and are increasing, they will keep you from being useless or unfruitful in the knowledge of our Lord Jesus Christ.

Peter lists for us the attributes we need to grow in as we walk with Christ. Developing these attributes is an ongoing process. The Word of God, the example of Christ and the Spirit of God help us walk through that process and increase in those areas. As we increase in those areas, we better reflect Christ's character, which is ultimately the kind of example we are called to be.

So what kind of example was Jesus? First and foremost, He was a servant leader. He knew exactly what His purpose was, and everything He did was tied to that purpose. He was a sacrifice. He was a redeemer—a restorer. Jesus lived in such a way as to challenge us to live the same kind of life before others.

As we strive to imitate that sacrificial example, we will attract the attention of those around us. Such actions speak loudly. They're so uncommon. As followers of Christ, that has to be who we are. Sacrifice and servanthood must become more common within our lives. Our actions must speak louder than our words.

TRAINING TIME

1. Who are some people in your life whose actions have spoken louder than words? What kind of impact, positive or negative, did they have on your life?

2. Why is it so important for leaders to live out their words rather than just talk a good game?
3. How would striving to follow Christ's example change your life and make you a more effective leader?

PRAYER

Father, remind me each morning before I go into the world that I am a living, breathing example of Your character to those around me. Give me the grace to not just talk the talk, but also walk the walk, and to be as Christlike in my actions as Your Spirit empowers me to be.

Clark Kellogg is the lead college basketball analyst for CBS Sports as well as the VP of player relations for the Indiana Pacers. He spent five years playing for the Pacers following a heralded career at Ohio State University, where he was the 1982 Big Ten Conference MVP.

Grace the Critics

MICHAEL CHANG

French Open Tennis Champion

Leading will undoubtedly bring criticism; handle with care.

The moment you step into a leadership role, you can be assured of one thing: You will face criticism. People will oppose you. Sometimes they will put you down because you're a threat to them. They may criticize you because they don't think you know what you're doing.

Leaders in this world are leaders because they're willing to take the risk to do something they're passionate about. If you're trying to make a difference in the world, you will be criticized.

I faced public criticism at the young age of 15, when I decided to make the leap from the junior tennis circuit to the professional ranks. I was just 5' 9" in shoes, and many questioned my rationale. One of my biggest critics was the late Arthur Ashe. He was someone I greatly respected as a legendary tennis champion and humanitarian. Arthur sent me a letter to explain why he thought turning professional would be a huge mistake for me. I know he had my best interests in mind, but it was still tough to hear such piercing words from someone I greatly admired.

Much later in my career as a professional, a feature article about Andre Agassi appeared in *GQ Magazine*. In the interview, Andre made some derogatory references to my Christian faith and commented that it was a joke for me to practice abstinence until I got married. He later apologized in a handwritten letter, but in the meantime, I was asked often about his remarks. The criticism turned into an opportunity for me to share my faith and explain how I wanted to honor God and my future wife.

In 1989, I experienced similar criticism, but on a much larger scale. That year, I fought through severe cramps in a fourth-round match against top-seeded Ivan Lendl after being down two sets to none. After the match was over, I told the French press that I won because of the Lord Jesus Christ. The following day, the media coverage was unbelievably negative. So was the audience response. When I walked onto the court and warmed up for each of my next three matches, the fans weren't just cheering for my opponent, they were actually rooting against me.

In the subsequent years I went back to Paris, I was greeted with boos and jeers. I called my dad after one of the matches and said, "You know what, Dad, I don't even want to come back to Paris and play again." It just wasn't fun anymore. Paris was the only place in the world where that was happening, and I was sick and tired of it.

My dad replied, "Michael, the Lord hasn't called you to just play in the places where people love you, support you and treat you well. The Lord called you to be a tennis player because you're a witness for Christ. It doesn't matter what kind of response you get. What's important is how you respond to it."

My dad's wisdom encouraged me to keep my sights set on Christ, and eventually, the crowds began to change. I still talked about my faith. I still signed my autographs, "Jesus loves you," but I did it with a better attitude. Incredibly, every time I went to Paris during the last five years of my career, the fans gave me the royal treatment and cheered for me as if I were one of their own.

In dealing with criticism, it's important to take each critique and look at it from an analytical perspective. Does the criticism have merit? Will the criticism actually help me? Sometimes criticism can be used in a positive way and spur you to become more focused and passionate about what you're trying to accomplish.

Evaluating criticism also keeps me from responding in the heat of the moment. If I react while I'm hot-headed, I'll end up saying things I regret because I spoke out of emotion. So I usually withdraw or take a walk and pray for guidance. If I need to give an immediate response, then I'll at least pause and give myself time to think before I speak.

I've learned so much about dealing with criticism by reading the Bible and seeing how Jesus reacted to the Pharisees when they constantly questioned His teachings. Jesus always responded with truth and love. Even when He was mocked, scorned, cursed at, beaten, spat on and finally crucified, Jesus never once lashed out at His accusers. He lived out His own words from Matthew 5:39 and turned the other cheek.

The disciples also endured criticism to the point of severe persecution and death. What I've had to deal with pales in comparison. They were martyrs for their faith. I might gripe sometimes about being criticized for what I believe, but in reality, I have nothing to complain about.

First Peter 4:12-14 confirms this truth and gives me hope in the midst of criticism:

> Dear friends, when the fiery ordeal arises among you to test you, don't be surprised by it, as if something unusual were happening to you. Instead, as you share in the sufferings of the Messiah rejoice, so that you may also rejoice with great joy at the revelation of His glory. If you are ridiculed for the name of Christ, you are blessed, because the Spirit of glory and of God rests on you.

The more grounded you are in the Word, the better off you're going to be. Then, when people criticize you, you'll be able to respond with a divine peace that is hard to describe. When my cup is full with the Spirit, I just don't get that irritated.

That's how I was able to deal with the critics in press conferences and interviews who attacked my faith. Those answers didn't come from me. Those words came from the Lord; I was just saying them out loud. He taught me how to do it His way rather than my way. And His way is always better.

TRAINING TIME

1. How often do you face criticism in your leadership position and for what issues?
2. What kinds of criticism challenge you the most? How do you usually respond to that criticism?
3. What can you learn from Jesus' response to criticism, and how can you apply that to your life?

PRAYER

Father, give me the wisdom to deal with criticism. If it is warranted, allow me to use it for my own good. If it is not warranted, give me the strength to show grace to my accusers.

Michael Chang is a retired tennis player who spent 15 years on the ATP tour. He won 34 career titles, including the 1989 French Open, which made him the youngest Grand Slam title winner. Chang is a member of the International Tennis Hall of Fame and now devotes his energy to the Chang Family Foundation.

Give It a Rest

SUE SEMRAU

Head Women's Basketball Coach, Florida State University

Leading is more effective when coupled with targeted times of solitude.

For today's college coach, long hours and seven-day workweeks are the rule, not the exception. At least that's what the world keeps telling me it takes to get ahead in this profession.

I bought into that system early in my career. As an assistant coach, I found myself losing focus easily and being distracted by very small things. My life was like a radio that couldn't pick up anything but static. I could constantly hear sounds, but it wasn't pleasant at all.

About 18 years ago, that all changed. At that time, the NCAA gave us 28 consecutive days for summer recruiting. I was in St. Louis with my good friend Julie Brown, now the head coach at Gordon College; as assistant coaches at Northern Illinois, we were several days into the recruiting process.

Worn down from the non-stop workload, Julie and I decided to pull out our Bibles and read about the Sabbath in an effort to justify our actions. As we took turns reading different passages, it became very clear that we could honor God or we could turn our heads. So right then and there, we decided to make a change. We took the day off and enjoyed some fun, rest and relaxation.

Sadly, there were really no coaches I could look to for an example of this principle. I had gone to clinic sessions and tried to read books on balance, yet nothing had seemed to work. On that day in St. Louis, we were literally two completely exhausted assistant coaches sitting down, reading God's Word and allowing God to clearly speak His truth into our hearts.

Once I started to schedule a Sabbath day into my week, my career really took off. My Sabbath wasn't always on Sunday, but it was always a day that was committed to rest. This principle became so important to me that when I got a head-coaching job, I made sure to put my staff on that same type of regimen. Initially, it was hard for those assistant coaches, but I'm convinced that following the principle of rest is one of the reasons our staff has been able to stay together and flourish the way we have.

In order to maintain this principle of rest, you have to be intentional. Look at every week in advance so you can wisely choose a day for your Sabbath. At Florida State, we are required to take a day off. That makes the most sense for our staff. We alert our support staff about which coach is going to be available at different times of the day if something happens. Then we stick to the plan.

Once it's time to rest, I'm usually so revved up that it takes me at least half a day before I can enjoy it. All of the junk that I have allowed into my heart during the week has to be purged. Those days of hard work aren't always as honoring to God as I'd like them to be. I let things come into my mind that have no business being there. But when I spend time with God, He removes the junk from my mind and heart. That's when I can really receive His rest. It's a very cleansing time for me.

Sometimes things happen and we are forced to shorten or delay our scheduled day of rest. In those times, you can't be completely legalistic. As Jesus said in Luke 14:5, "Which of you whose son or ox falls into a well, will not immediately pull him out on the Sabbath day?" Jesus spoke those words right after He healed a man in front of the Pharisees on the Jewish day of rest.

As committed as I've been to this principle over the years, there are still moments when I feel uptight about taking a day off. That's when I go back and remind myself of God's command to honor the Sabbath. I let those Scriptures refresh me and wash over my heart and my mind. Isaiah 58:13-14 gives us this promise:

> If you keep from desecrating the Sabbath, from doing whatever you want on My holy day; if you call the Sabbath a delight, and the holy [day] of the LORD honorable; if you honor it, not going your own ways, seeking your own pleasure, or talking too much; then you will delight yourself in the LORD, and I will make you ride over the heights of the land, and let you enjoy the heritage of your father Jacob.

This passage reinforces the truth that God will honor those who make time to rest in Him and bless them with renewed minds and refreshed bodies.

In Matthew 5:17, Jesus tells us that He didn't come to destroy the Law but to fulfill it. Proof of this claim can be found in the way He embraced and honored the Sabbath tradition. Jesus routinely took that day to worship and teach at the temple. He also spent time in solitude and communion with His Father. Because of that commitment, Jesus always had peace in times when He could have been very agitated.

If even Jesus needed to get away and clear His mind of the static and noise that bombarded Him, how much more do we need that time of rest and solitude? I desperately need the peace that comes from my Sabbath. I can only imagine that many other coaches and leaders, with all the pressures they face, need to experience it too.

I would encourage anyone to work really hard and go after whatever it is you're trying to accomplish, but then obey God and take that time of rest and solitude. When you do that, He'll give you the strength to work harder, better and smarter.

TRAINING TIME

1. How often do you take time away? What does that time look like?
2. On a scale of 1-10, how effective do you feel after you've had targeted times of rest and solitude? How does your effectiveness rank when you've gone long periods of time without a break?
3. What steps can you take this week to plan a Sabbath day into your schedule?

PRAYER

Father, reveal to me the importance of giving You significant amounts of my time in rest and solitude. Give me the practical tools to implement a Sabbath day by which I can honor You and in turn receive strength, renewal and peace.

Sue Semrau is the head women's basketball coach at Florida State University and has won the most games of any coach in the school's history. Through the 2011 season, she has led the Seminoles to eight NCAA Tournament appearances, including an active streak of seven. Under Semrau, Florida State has twice tied for first place in the Atlantic Coast Conference (2009 and 2010). Her team reached the Elite Eight in 2010 with a 29-6 record.

28

Trust God

JOHN SHELBY

Coach, Milwaukee Brewers

Leading is an exercise in faith.

For the past 33 years, I've suited up in a baseball uniform at the professional level—first as a player and now as a coach. Only once have I had a two-year contract. The rest of the time, I've worked each year with no guarantee of a job the following season.

If that's not faith and if that's not trust, then I don't know what trust is. I honestly believe that God created us with a purpose for a purpose. I haven't always been where I want to be, but I know I'm where He wants me to be. That's where I find my contentment and peace. When my contract expires at the end of the season, I pray and ask the Lord to put me on someone's heart. I know that He has a place for me, so I just trust and wait on Him.

Trusting in God is a principle by which all Christians, especially Christian leaders, should live. I've learned to trust God in every situation and every circumstance. I've even learned to trust Him in areas where I think I might have control, because I want Him to be first and foremost in my life. Everything that has happened to me—my wife, my family, my career, everything—is from

God. I want to make sure that I trust in God as I lead and that He gets all the glory and honor.

One of the verses that reminds me of this principle is Proverbs 3:5-6: "Trust in the LORD with all your heart, and do not rely on your own understanding; think about Him in all your ways, and He will guide you on the right paths." One of these instances of God guiding my path occurred at the end of the 2007 baseball season when my contract expired with the Pittsburgh Pirates. The team was in the process of hiring a new manager and coaching staff, so I contacted various teams in search of a new job for the 2008 season. Nothing seemed to be opening up.

A couple of weeks later, my wife, Trina, and I were walking through our neighborhood. As we walked, I prayed for my previous staff members and asked the Lord to bless them with jobs before praying for myself. As we finished up and walked back into our home, the phone rang. Trina answered, handed the phone to me, and said it was someone named Dave who wanted to speak to me. He introduced himself, but I knew who he was. He said that he was looking for a first-base/outfield coach, and for some reason he had me on his mind. After talking for a while, he offered me the job, and I gladly accepted. I told Trina that Dave was the manager of the Baltimore Orioles, which was one of the teams that I did not call when I was searching for a job. Trina and I looked at each other, laughed, and praised God for putting me on Dave's mind.

During those uncertain times, it would have been easy to worry about not having a job. It could have been tempting to try to make things happen on my own. But like the Proverb says, we can't trust what we see with our natural eyes, because we can't see what He sees. Often just in the moment when we're about to lose hope, God comes through and puts us right where we need to be. I am a witness to that truth.

Jesus gave us the perfect illustration of this principle. Even though His flesh longed for another way to fulfill God's plan for salvation as He cried out, "My Father! If it is possible, let this cup pass from Me," Jesus trusted the Father and prayed, "Yet not as I will, but as You will" (Matthew 26:39).

That's the standard I want to use for my life as a leader in the clubhouse, in my church and in my family. If I can trust Him and believe what His Word says, I know that regardless of the outcome, things are going to work out for my best.

TRAINING TIME

1. In what areas of your life do you find it easy to trust God? In what parts of your life do you find it difficult?
2. Can you think of a time when trusting God in a difficult situation worked out to your benefit?
3. What are some things you can do today to start trusting God with all aspects of your life?

PRAYER

Father, help me place my full confidence and trust in You. Just as Solomon wrote in Proverbs, teach me to lean on Your wisdom and not on my own understanding. Give me the faith to follow the path You have paved before me.

John Shelby is a coach with the Milwaukee Brewers and has previously served in that capacity with the Los Angeles Dodgers, Pittsburgh Pirates and Baltimore Orioles. As a player, Shelby spent 11 years in the Majors as a member of the Orioles, Dodgers and Detroit Tigers. He was a key member of two World Series champion teams: Baltimore (1983) and Los Angeles (1988). Shelby serves on the ministry staff at his hometown church in Lexington, Kentucky.

29

Lose the Weights

JIM RYUN

Olympic Silver Medalist, Track and Field

Leading with transparency requires a heart of forgiveness.

The Lord calls those of us in leadership to be transparent and pure in heart. But if we're carrying bitterness or anger, we will not have healthy relationships with those we're leading or, more importantly, with God. I had to come to grips with this principle while lying on a track, watching my competitors speed across the finish line.

My story starts on May 18, 1972, when my wife, Anne, and I accepted Christ as our Savior and Lord. Less than four months later, I was in Munich, Germany, preparing to run the 1,500-meter race at the Olympics. In my heart, I wanted to win the gold medal for the glory of God. I wanted to get on the top of that podium and use my victory as a platform to share the gospel with others. But God saw a better way.

After winning the silver medal four years earlier in Mexico City, I was considered the favorite to win gold in my third and final Olympic appearance. In the preliminary round, there was a lap and a half to go when the unthinkable happened. Another runner, Billy Fordjour of Ghana, bumped my trail leg, and I tripped and fell down. I lay on the track, stunned, only for a few seconds, but enough time passed that when I got up to finish the race, I missed advancing to the next round of competition.

I got off the track and met my wife in the tunnel. Anne and I embraced each other and prayed, asking God, "What do we do now?" We had made the decision to honor Him, but we didn't know if that meant going forward with the petition for reinstatement or gracefully moving on from a chance for Olympic gold.

We decided to submit the petition and wait to see what was going to happen. I was warming up the next day when the official informed me of his decision. He looked at me and said, "You know, Jim, what happened to you is really unfortunate. But we've never reinstated anybody at this point in an Olympic competition. Why don't you come back in four years and try again?"

I was a young Christian and knew I needed to do the right thing, but I wanted to reach out and grab him by his tie and pound on him a little bit with my fist so he could feel some of the pain that I was feeling. There was no way he could have understood the hundreds of miles of training in all kinds of weather, or the traveling and sacrifices my wife and I had made over the last four years to pursue this dream. To have that official dismiss me in such a cavalier way really hurt me.

Slowly, over a period of time, I realized that I was angry and very bitter because I didn't get my way. I had been like Santa Claus, carrying a big bag over my shoulders—except my bag wasn't full of toys. It was weighing me down with pity, blame, anger and grief. Carrying that bag was a way of justifying my hurt feelings.

That sack of junk slows many people down. Like I was back then, they're willing to carry around things from the past they may not even know they're carrying. Once they let go of those things, there's tremendous relief that takes them back to the feeling they had when they first met the Lord. That's what forgiveness does. It lets you move from being underneath a burden to being free in the Lord. That's the message found in Hebrews 12:1, in which the apostle Paul tells us to "lay aside every weight and the sin that so easily ensnares us."

The most dangerous byproduct of an unforgiving spirit is identified in Matthew 6:15. In that passage, Jesus warns, "But if you don't forgive people, your Father will not forgive your wrongdoing." Forgiveness is ultimately a conditional process. It's imperative that we do what's necessary to participate in the process.

As leaders, it's essential that we live a life that embraces this principle of forgiveness. Matthew 18:22 records Jesus' response to Peter's question about how often we are to forgive others: "'I tell you, not as many as seven,' Jesus said to him, 'but 70 times seven.'"

The number 490 wasn't given so you'll never stop forgiving someone. Jesus was simply illustrating that as you keep forgiving, at some point, it becomes a lot easier to stop holding a grudge. Forgiveness isn't necessarily a one-time situation. It's something you have to work on constantly. Peter was looking for a finite approach, and Jesus pointed out that it's an ongoing process.

As I study the concept of forgiveness, it becomes very clear to me that Jesus is continually giving us the opportunity to make amends. He does this because He loves us so much. Forgiveness is a love process. It's a choice you make that leads to a brighter relationship. It goes both ways. You have to be willing to forgive, and then God is able to do great things as a result of your choice to open up and deal with your hurts.

I learned that process from my own journey of forgiveness. My family and I attended the Los Angeles Olympics in 1984, 12 years after the incident in Munich. We were at the Coliseum for the final day of track and field, with all of the glamour events like the 1,500-meter run and the marathon. We sat in a very high section, and it was hard to see things on the ground.

From my vantage point, the athletes looked like ants, so I watched the pole vault competition on the video screen. As I watched,

I spotted a familiar face next to one of the athletes. It was that same official who in 1972 could have reinstated me. I turned to Anne and said, "Back in 1972, I wanted to punch that man, but now I want to share the gospel with him."

Forgiveness is something you deal with on a daily basis. Having served in public office, I've had many opportunities to forgive people for things they have said about me. Some meant to hurt me, and others didn't, but both required me to grow within the process. As leaders, it is gravely important that we practice the principle of forgiveness every moment of each day. Only then will we be effective at our posts and able to walk transparently and purely before God.

TRAINING TIME

1. Are you struggling to forgive someone for something they did to hurt you?
2. How has unforgiveness impacted your ability to lead?
3. What steps do you need to take to forgive that person and begin the process of moving forward with freedom in Christ?

PRAYER

Father, show me the pockets of my heart where I've been hiding bitterness and unforgiveness towards another. Grant me the mercy to forgive and the grace to leave those hurts in the past.

Jim Ryun is a three-time track Olympian who won the 1,500-meter silver medal at the 1968 Summer Olympics in Mexico City. He is the former holder of five world records and a five-time NCAA Champion. He was named High School Athlete of the Century by ESPN over Tiger Woods and LeBron James. Ryun served in the U.S. House of Representatives from 1996 to 2007, representing his home state of Kansas, and is the author of *The Courage to Run.*

Don't Be So Humble (You're Not that Great)

TONY BENNETT

Head Men's Basketball Coach, University of Virginia

Leading with humility takes sober self-judgment.

My dad is Dick Bennett. He's a retired basketball coach who had a successful career at places like Wisconsin, Washington State and Wisconsin-Green Bay. Dad used to quote this funny saying that is usually credited to Golda Meir, Israel's first female Prime Minister: "Don't be so humble. You're not that great."

When I first heard that, my instinct was to tilt my head and curiously raise my eyebrow. But as I let the irony of the statement sink in, its powerful message took root in my heart. Humility is, in fact, one of the great biblical conundrums, but it's also a principle that can make or break a leader.

I've always been drawn to leaders who are humble. David Robinson and Mark Price were two of my basketball heroes, and great Christian leaders such as Billy Graham and Mother Teresa also had significant influence on me and my leadership style.

By watching those people and my dad, I gained an understanding of what humility looks like. They modeled the definition of humility found in Romans 12:3: "Do not think of yourself more highly than you ought, but rather think of yourself with sober judgment, in accordance with the faith God has distributed to each of you" (*TNIV*).

As a player, I was fortunate enough to play in college and have a short NBA career. I went through the ranks, trying to reach the highest level. It's easy to get a little puffed up after experiencing some success. I remember as a player thinking I was pretty great after having a good game, but then the next time out I'd get my lunch handed to me. Those are humbling experiences. In the sports arena, you have to have strength and confidence, but if you become conceited or overconfident, the competition serves as a truth serum.

The same is true now that I'm a coach. I remember my second year as an assistant coach under my father at Washington State. A group of freshmen had been brought in to turn the program around. We played an Oklahoma State team that had played in the Final Four the previous season. We went to Stillwater and got beat, 81-29. That experience stripped everything away. When you are truly humbled, it really does bring you to your knees and cause you to say, "Lord, what am I going to do now?"

That loss was the catalyst for what was to come. When those freshmen became juniors and seniors, they finished second in the Pac-10 one year and third the other year. They were ranked in the top 10 and made it to a Sweet 16. No one thought they were ever going to build a program. But it was that humbling experience and adversity that caused our team to work.

A life of humility brings so many wonderful benefits. You're standing on solid ground when you're genuine, and you have an understanding of who you are and what matters. You're not as reliant upon what others think or say. There is a peace and a foundation upon which you can stand.

Humility also allows you to keep things in proper perspective. Instead of taking all of the credit for your success, you are empowered to share the moment with your teammates and others who have helped you along the way. Most importantly, humility makes it easier for you to give the glory to God, who ultimately deserves it all anyway.

When humility is absent, however, you're setting yourself up for a tumble. In Proverbs 18:12, Solomon tells us, "Before his downfall a man's heart is proud." When you start thinking it's about your own strength, your own power, or your own abilities and skills, there will eventually come a downfall.

Humility isn't an easy characteristic to attain. As you strive to be more humble, you first have to know your strengths and your weaknesses. From there, you constantly have to check yourself and ask yourself hard questions.

The more time you spend in the Word and with God, the more you grow in your faith. You begin to realize how amazing God is and how flawed you are. As your faith in Christ deepens, you'll be blown away by what He accomplished at the cross. If that doesn't humble you—realizing who you were before you had a relationship with Christ, and recognizing the enormity of what He did for you—then not much will.

God's Word also gives us the most incredible example of humility in the life of Christ. He Himself instructs in Matthew 11:29: "Learn from Me, because I am gentle and humble in heart, and you will find rest for yourselves."

What can we as leaders learn from Christ's humility? In Philippians 2:5-8, the apostle Paul tells us to take on His attitude, which "did not consider equality with God as something to be used for His own advantage" (verse 6). Paul goes on to write that Jesus "emptied Himself by assuming the form of a slave" (verse 7) and was "obedient to the point of death—even to death on a cross" (verse 8).

Jesus knew His purpose. He was about His Father's business. Even when He was insulted, mocked, tortured and ridiculed, He never strayed from His mission. He knew the end of the story and what was needed to save humankind.

That's our example and the standard for which all Christian leaders should reach. Then, when you think you've arrived, quickly realize that you haven't. As Golda Meir said, "Don't be so humble, you're not that great."

TRAINING TIME

1. In what areas of your life do you struggle with humility? Are there any areas where you lack confidence or think "too lowly" of yourself?
2. Have you ever experienced a "downfall" such as Solomon refers to in Proverbs 18:12?
3. What does the saying, "Don't be so humble, you're not that great" mean to you?

PRAYER

Father, humble my heart. Help me not to think too highly of myself, but also not to think too lowly. Let me see myself in the same way You see me.

Tony Bennett is the head men's basketball coach at the University of Virginia. He was previously the head coach at Washington State, where he led the Cougars to two NCAA Tournament appearances (including a Sweet 16 in 2008) and was named the AP Coach of the Year in 2007. Bennett played collegiately at Wisconsin-Green Bay and is still the NCAA record holder for career three-point shooting percentage (.497). He spent three seasons in the NBA with the Charlotte Hornets.

31

Great Leaders Teach

MIKE SINGLETARY

Assistant NFL Head Coach; Super Bowl Champion

Leading is about sharing your experience and modeling it to others.

Teaching is a requirement for all great leaders. I've had tremendous teachers in my lifetime. They weren't always speaking when they were teaching, but the message was so loud, I can still hear it.

My first teacher was my mom, Rudell Singletary. When I was 12 years old, my parents got divorced. As the last of ten kids, I suddenly found myself the beneficiary of my mom's undivided attention. After school or football practice, we would sit at the kitchen table, and she would teach me lessons based on the Bible, her personal experience, or practical things I needed to know. She poured her life into me.

When I went to Baylor, my head coach was an outstanding man named Grant Teaff. I learned so much through his example. He taught me the value of mentoring. He showed an interest in every aspect of my life. He invited me into his home, where I saw how he handled his family affairs. Coach Teaff also taught me what it meant to conduct myself as a Christian athlete.

One of the teachers who influenced me most was in the classroom, not on the field. I hated English, but as a freshman I was required to take an English class. Everything I heard from the upperclassmen was, "Whatever you do, don't get Ann Miller! She's crazy!" They told me she didn't like athletes, and she especially didn't like black athletes. By the time I was able to pick my classes, Ann Miller was the only English professor available. I was determined to take 15 hours, so I decided to enroll in the course.

The first day, she gave the class an assignment that I was not prepared to do. I was trying to make the football team, and I was in biology classes as a pre-med student. I had to make a choice between a biology assignment and the English assignment. I decided to focus on biology and use whatever time I had left to work on English.

When she was returning our papers, she turned mine face down and said, "Mr. Singletary, I don't know where you're from. I don't know why you chose this class. But I want you to understand this: Don't you ever come to this class again unprepared! Do you understand what I'm saying?" She said this loudly, and everybody was looking at me.

"Yes, ma'am, I understand," I replied.

Then she turned my paper over and revealed that I had received an F. "If you want to talk to me about this, I'll be available for a short time after class."

After class, I explained to her my situation. She replied, "This is college. I understand that you have 15 hours. If you have to drop this class, drop this class. But I want you to know that I expect you to give your best in this class, and nothing other than that is accepted. As long as you understand that, I will help you every way that I can. But don't you ever come through that door unprepared and not ready to learn and give me your absolute best."

From that day on, I would go to her after class and she would spend time working with me. About midway through the semester, she had me so excited about English that I almost changed my major. Her enthusiasm made me believe that English was wonderful. I loved her because of that. I was so shy coming into that class, yet she eventually had me standing on top of my desk shouting, "To be or not to be!"

Ann Miller made me understand that it's not so much about the class—it's about the teacher. The teacher has a responsibility to make a connection with the student. That's what Ann Miller did for this African-American kid who started out hating English but grew to love it because I loved her. We remained friends and, up until her passing in 2006, I would go back to Waco and visit her. She meant that much to me. She changed my life.

Sometimes teachers aren't people. They are circumstances we face in life. One of the greatest teachers is failure. In those times, a wise person will say, "How do I take this negative and make it into a positive?" My teachers have taught me that failure can be a blessing if you embrace it for what it's worth and then let it go and move on. Some of the greatest people in life became great after they failed.

When I was fired as the San Francisco 49ers' head coach, I was squarely faced with this hard lesson. I had to choose between becoming bitter and becoming better. I had to decide whether or not I was going to trust God. I chose to trust Him. I didn't like being in the valley, but I understood that it's part of the journey. I refused to let anyone put a period at that juncture.

Ultimately, no other teacher compares to Christ. The greatest lessons I've learned about teaching have come from reading about His life. The words He spoke challenge me every day. Jesus was often addressed as "teacher" or "Rabbi," which was a show of respect from those seeking His counsel and wisdom. People knew they were hearing from the Master when He spoke to them.

Jesus' command in Matthew 4:19, "Follow Me," is very simple, yet this is something that is very hard for leaders to do. But as we follow Jesus Christ, we are better equipped to lead others. I have to be the example and teach my players or my children the right way to go by doing it myself.

Learning and teaching are all about what you have to give. It is important to me to learn about three things: my faith in Jesus Christ, how to be a great husband and a great dad, and everything I can about coaching. The more I learn, the more I have to give to my students, and the better it is for them. As a leader, that should be the focus: serving and teaching the ones you are leading, and empowering them to fulfill their God-given destiny.

TRAINING TIME

1. What teachers have had the greatest influence in your life? What did you learn from them?
2. In what ways can you improve your knowledge and wisdom in order to be a better teacher?
3. Who are some people in your circle of influence whom you can begin teaching today?

PRAYER

Father, give me the heart of a teacher. Help me to see how I might influence those around me by pouring into them the knowledge and wisdom other teachers have poured into my life.

Mike Singletary is the assistant head coach for the Minnesota Vikings. He previously was the head coach for the San Francisco 49ers. He spent 12 seasons playing linebacker for the Chicago Bears; during those years, he was selected for 10 Pro Bowls and led the team to the Super Bowl XX championship. Singletary, a member of both the College and Pro Football Halls of Fame, is also a motivational speaker and the author of three books, including *Mike Singletary One-on-One* (with Jay Carty).

32

Sharpen the Axe

JEREMY AFFELDT
MLB Pitcher

Lead with spiritual adeptness.

As a Christian ballplayer, I've learned that there comes a time when you've got to act like a Christian ballplayer. Among other things, that means you go all out and work really hard at what you do. I didn't always have this mindset, though.

It's taken me many years to get to this level of spiritual adeptness, and I still have a long way to go. As a military family, we traveled all over the country while I was growing up, and at one point we were stationed in Guam. My parents were Christians, but it was a challenge to settle into a community of believers. We would go to whatever church was around, and that exposed me to different philosophies, different theologies and different ways of worship.

As a high school athlete, I struggled greatly with my attitude. I played basketball at Northwest Christian High School in Colbert, Washington, and at one point my head coach, Danny Duke, benched me as a way of getting my attention. I quickly straightened up because I didn't want basketball to be taken away from me. But my heart still needed to change.

In 1997, the Kansas City Royals drafted me straight out of high school. My girlfriend, Larisa (who would later become my wife), gave me a Bible to help me deal with the process. I went to Florida to play summer ball, and after the games, I just sat in my hotel room. I was 18 years old and scared to death. I'd never been away from my family before. Not knowing what else to do, I started reading the Bible Larisa had given me. The more I read, the more interested I became. I bought books about the Christian faith, and eventually I gained confidence in my personal beliefs. My faith became my own.

Five years later, I won a spot in the Royals' bullpen. Since then, I've played for the Cincinnati Reds, the Colorado Rockies and the San Francisco Giants, where I was blessed to be a part of the 2010 World Series champion team. Just as I've had to adjust to different clubhouses, I have also dealt with changing roles. I've been a starter, a reliever and a closer, but one role I've had from the beginning as a Christian athlete is the role of a leader.

I know that I'm performing for the One who created me as His perfect workmanship. As Christians, we play for the audience of One, so whether we're athletes, coaches, students or at any other station in life, we should work hard using the gifts He has given us. That's a sign of biblical leadership.

That's why it's so important for me to live by the truth found in Ecclesiastes 10:10. King Solomon wrote, "If the axe is dull, and one does not sharpen its edge, then one must exert more strength; however, the advantage of wisdom is that it brings success."

If I want to succeed, I need to keep my axe sharp at all times. In this passage, the word "axe" can be interpreted many ways. In the natural, sharpening my axe means that when I get to the field, I think only about baseball and concentrate on my skills.

I ask lots of questions of my fellow players and our coaches about how to improve. I also ask God to show me things on the mound that I need to do better. I even ask Him to teach me how to pitch. He understands how it all works. When I take advantage of His wisdom, "it brings success."

In the spiritual realm, sharpening my axe means getting into His Word and spending time in prayer. It also means keeping my eyes open for opportunities to serve my teammates. If someone wants a bottle of water, I try to get it for him. When in conversation with others, I ask how their families are doing. I encourage them when they're dealing with issues both on and off the field. I do these things so that I might be a living example of the gospel.

Again, having a sharp axe and using Christ's wisdom will bring success. We can't become islands. We can't be a reflection of Jesus if we're hiding ourselves from others. We have to be around non-believers. However, we also have to be built up in our faith. I'll go out and eat with the guys, but if they want to do things that I don't think are morally correct, I just go back to the hotel. They know that I'm approachable, but they also know that I don't compromise my values.

Christ is the perfect example of a man who daily sharpened His axe. He prayed, He read the Scriptures, He fasted and He sacrificially gave of Himself to all who crossed His path. This way of life is also taught in Ephesians 5:8-9, where the apostle Paul wrote, "For you were once darkness, but now [you are] light in the Lord. Walk as children of light—for the fruit of the light [results] in all goodness, righteousness, and truth."

That brief passage of Scripture sums up how we as Christians need to be living in this world. We need to be truthful, righteous and living our lives according to His Word and in a way that shows God's love and goodness to all people. There's no way to do those things without daily sharpening our axes.

TRAINING TIME

1. What does "sharpening the axe" look like to you in your natural life and your spiritual life?
2. What are some areas in the natural and spiritual realms where your axe could stand sharpening?
3. What are some steps that you can begin taking today that will help sharpen those areas, and what might success look like as you become more spiritually adept?

PRAYER

Father, help me daily to sharpen my axe—those tools and talents that You've given me to use for Your glory. I desire Your wisdom that comes as I draw closer to You through the exercise of spiritual disciplines. I want to be an instrument of love and truth that can be used to reach those around me with the gospel of salvation and hope.

Jeremy Affeldt is a pitcher with the San Francisco Giants. Originally drafted by the Kansas City Royals, he has also played in Colorado and Cincinnati. In 2007, Affeldt made his first World Series appearance with the National League Champion Rockies. In 2010, he was a member of San Francisco's World Series champion team.

Persist with Purpose

JEAN DRISCOLL

Paralympic and Boston Marathon Champion Wheelchair Racer

Leading through adversity takes principled perseverance.

I know a thing or two about perseverance. I have lived out this principle starting as a young child and into adulthood as a notable wheelchair racer. Perseverance is an unwavering, purposeful persistence that continues in both good times and bad.

I was born in Milwaukee, Wisconsin, with spina bifida or "open spine." Back in the mid-1960s, nearly half of the babies born with this condition died from infection or other complications. Even though my spina bifida was milder than some cases, I still wore leg braces to help me walk. My balance wasn't very good. My feet turned out to the side, and I would sway back and forth. There were many people who tried to place limitations on my life, but deep inside, I knew I was capable of more, so I didn't give up.

The ups and downs of my life may epitomize perseverance, but I am amazed at the people and circumstances God has used to teach me something new about persistence, dedication and purpose.

Marty Morse, my track coach at the University of Illinois, continually badgered me about competing in a marathon. I was fearful of the distance and had no interest in doing a marathon. After winning my first national road race at the Bloomsday in Spokane, Washington, I finally gave in to Marty's request. At the Chicago Marathon in October 1989, my goal was to keep up with my teammates. Surprisingly, I finished second in a time of 1:59:52. My heart sank when Marty informed me that I had qualified for the Boston Marathon.

After losing one of the wheels from the racing chair during the Los Angeles Marathon, I was dreading going to Boston. But Marty kept pushing me and telling me I could do it. I didn't realize it at the time, but God had placed something inside of my heart that gave me the strength to put in the hard work and long hours of training necessary to be successful at an elite level.

When the race started, I was among the first three women to break away from the pack. Then I pulled ahead of the girl who had won the Boston Marathon and broken the world record the year before. When I crossed the finish line, not only did I win my first Boston Marathon, but I also broke the world record by almost seven minutes. The "runner's high" lasted for weeks!

Imagine if I hadn't persevered through my doubts and fears. What if I had given up after a few bad training sessions or my awful experience in Los Angeles? I would have fallen short of my goal to be excellent. Even worse, I wouldn't have reached the potential God planted within me, and I wouldn't have had a chance to encounter some amazing people in Ghana, West Africa.

In 2001, I traveled to Ghana for the first time with Joni Eareckson Tada's ministry, Joni and Friends, to teach at a wheelchair track camp. As prospective athletes with disabilities began arriving at the track, some limped into the stadium, while others walked with crutches. Only a few of them had their own wheelchairs.

The most surprising moments came, however, when several people crawled into the stadium wearing sandals on their hands.

They had crawled two or three blocks from their hostel to reach the track. Even though each person was only able to be up off the ground while they had their turn in the donated racing chairs, they prayed and sang praise songs with heartfelt exuberance before each workout. Needless to say, their perseverance and love for God was inspiring.

Those beautiful people in Africa reminded me that perseverance yields joy and then, consequently, joy yields perseverance. Without either of them, the challenges before us seem greater than they really are. There is joy and purpose when living with perseverance. Few excuses are made because the desire to succeed is a driving force.

A powerful promise of God's strength for the benefit of our perseverance is found in Isaiah 40:28-31:

> Do you not know? Have you not heard? Yahweh is the everlasting God, the Creator of the whole earth. He never grows faint or weary; there is no limit to His understanding. He gives strength to the weary and strengthens the powerless. Youths may faint and grow weary, and young men stumble and fall, but those who trust in the LORD will renew their strength; they will soar on wings like eagles; they will run and not grow weary; they will walk and not faint.

Winston Churchill once said, "A pessimist sees the difficulty in every opportunity; an optimist sees the opportunity in every difficulty." It's that kind of perspective that leads to perseverance and to the completion of whatever work God has begun in us.

Jesus had that perspective. He saw the whole picture. He knew where the finish line was, and He understood what was waiting there. That's why Jesus was a leader who led with His eyes toward heaven. He told His disciples honestly, "In this world you will have trouble. But take heart! I have overcome the world" (John 16:33, *NIV*). His messages of faith, hope and love, even in the midst of His own struggles and suffering, provide important illustrations of perseverance and continue to inspire people from all walks of life today.

As leaders, it is our job to inspire people to persevere through adversity so they too can reach the finish line and experience their full potential. But that can't happen until we first learn the value of perseverance in our own lives.

TRAINING TIME

1. What is the biggest adversity you've faced in your life? How did you push yourself to persevere through that challenge?
2. How have your obstacles turned into opportunities to impact others?
3. What Christlike attributes might help you persevere until you've reached your goals as a leader?

PRAYER

Father, show me my purpose and then grant me the perseverance to overcome any obstacles that this world might set in my way. I want to reach the finish line and also lead others there for Your glory.

Jean Driscoll is a four-time Paralympic athlete who won 12 medals, including five gold medals. She won a record-setting seven consecutive Boston Marathons in the wheelchair division en route to her also record-setting eight career victories. Driscoll won silver medals at the 1992 and 1996 Summer Olympics in exhibition competition. Now retired from racing, Driscoll is the Associate Director of Development for the College of Applied Health Sciences at the University of Illinois. She is a member of FCA's Hall of Champions and the Wheelchair Sports USA Hall of Fame.

Consistency Makes You Better

LORENZO ROMAR

Head Men's Basketball Coach, University of Washington

Leading with consistency is the difference between good and great.

There are a lot of good basketball coaches at the NCAA Division I level, but I am convinced that consistency is what makes a good coach great. I am sure of this because two of my mentors—John Wooden and Jim Harrick—were both great coaches and models of consistency.

As a young assistant coach at UCLA, I worked under Coach Harrick, who taught me how to organize and maximize a practice. To this day, I go back during the season and review the progress our team has made, as well as the pace at which those improvements came. This allows me to see how a consistent approach to teaching fundamentals and various offensive and defensive schemes has paid off in the development of our players.

During my time at UCLA and later as the head coach of Pepperdine, I also experienced Coach Wooden's notoriously consistent coaching style. In my cherished meetings with him, I was awed by the way he treated people consistently and truly gave of himself. Year in and year out, his players knew exactly what to expect from him and his staff. Even more importantly, Coach Wooden was consistent in his character and in his faith walk. Consistency is undoubtedly a key principle that opens the doors to success.

The bottom line is that consistency makes you better. A big part of consistency is preparation. I must admit, however, that I tend to be somewhat impulsive. I may hit something hard for three days and then forget about it for two weeks. That's a flaw and something upon which I've had to work hard to improve.

As my consistency as a coach has gotten stronger, I've begun to reap some of its benefits. For instance, whether or not people agree with your rules or your way of doing things, if you're consistent, they learn to respect them. They know what to expect. You must be consistent not only in what you demand, but also in how you yourself perform.

Consistency breeds a sense of value. When you're a leader, people look to see what is important to you. You may believe something's really important, but if that's not what you're demanding from your players every day, it won't be very important to the ones following you. Consistency sends this message: "If we're always doing this, then this is really important to Coach."

Inconsistent leadership will hinder your team's ability to perform well over the long haul. If people don't know what to expect from your leadership, the result is confusion. In the sports world, there's a comfort level and a rhythm that individual players and teams need to have. If you don't have a consistent approach, your players are never really comfortable. They don't quite get into a rhythm. The same is true for people who work in an office or any team environment. It's hard to know what to do if the boss hasn't laid out consistent expectations.

As someone who has struggled with consistency, I've learned to take steps to improve that area of my life. As a coach, I surround myself with people who are willing to help keep me accountable. I also write everything down. I take notes when I listen to someone speak, or when I read a book. Then I take notes on my notes to explain my thoughts. You must concentrate on the details in order to maintain a high level of consistency.

When I'm able to refer back to earlier ideas and methods and determine whether or not they were successful, a pattern begins to form, and the stage for consistency is set. I truly believe that it was the consistency of our staff that helped our 2009 team reach its full potential and ultimately win the Pac-10 Championship. I also believe that the consistent teaching of teamwork has made our program an exemplary model of unselfish basketball.

The foundation for consistency can be found in God's Word. In the book of Daniel, for instance, we read about Daniel's custom of praying three times a day in his window where everyone could see. Daniel remained faithful to that routine even when he knew he would be tossed into the lions' den for going against the king's decree.

From the Bible we also learn that Jesus went to the synagogue every Sabbath. It was His custom to get up early every morning and pray before He did anything else. He was the perfect model of consistency. His disciples knew what to expect from Him. Jesus had a vision, and He did not deviate from the script. In a three and a half year period, He set out to serve and ultimately save mankind, and He never got off the path.

I would never claim to be the most consistent coach, but I do know that the Holy Spirit is daily challenging me to be more consistent—and that the more consistent I am, the better it is for my team. With Jesus as my example and His Word as my guide, I will continue to strive for the kind of consistent life as a coach, husband, father and man of God that will draw others to Him.

TRAINING TIME

1. In what areas of your life are you consistent, and in what areas do you struggle with consistency?
2. What are the fruits you've personally experienced from a consistent life? What about the fruits of inconsistency?
3. What steps do you need to take to become more consistent as a leader, believer and family member?

PRAYER

Father, I want to live a consistent, faithful life that pleases You. Holy Spirit, convict me of those areas where I lack consistency and give me the tools, through Your Word and through others around me, to step out in faith onto a new path of consistent living.

Lorenzo Romar is the head men's basketball coach at his alma mater, the University of Washington. He spent five years playing in the NBA before embarking on a coaching career that has included stops at UCLA (where he was an assistant coach on the 1995 national championship team), Pepperdine and Saint Louis University. Romar has led Washington to six NCAA Tournament appearances, a Pac-10 regular season title and three Pac-10 Tournament titles. Romar is also a two-time Pac-10 Coach of the Year.

Give It All for the Team

BRIAN KINCHEN

Retired NFL Tight End and Long Snapper;
Super Bowl Champion

Leading selflessly sets the tone for teamwork.

Teamwork is the essential element of success in life. That might sound like a cliché coming from a high school football coach, but there is much more depth in that principle than we as leaders sometimes recognize.

My main goal as a coach is to teach my players the concept of teamwork. Not only does it benefit the team's performance, but it also sets the stage for every aspect of life, including marriage, employment, education, parenting and faith. It's a principle that is foundational to everything else you're trying to teach: commitment, accountability, hard work, discipline and intensity.

I didn't recognize the true value of teamwork until my junior year at University High School in Baton Rouge, Louisiana. We were a small, 1A team and I was one of the most decorated players. That year we got a new coach named Willis Stelly. He was all about the team. My previous coach was excellent, but he tended to cater to me and treat me differently.

When Coach Stelly came in, everyone was treated equally. That frustrated me. I thought I was supposed to be different. I was the one who was making the plays. It took me awhile, but I finally began to grasp what teamwork was all about. Years later, I was able to look back and be thankful to have a coach who was tough enough to instill that value in me.

I experienced something similar when, after nearly two years away from the game, I received the opportunity to join the New England Patriots late in the 2003 season. Even though I only played in five games, I experienced a cohesiveness and unity unlike anything I'd known before in my 13 years in the NFL. The attitude of teamwork permeated the entire organization. On my first day there, Tom Brady and Tedy Bruschi both welcomed me to the team. They set the tone for what was expected of everyone. They didn't just preach hard work and accountability—they lived it out.

Just like Brady and Bruschi, coaches and leaders must display teamwork through actions, not just words. First, your players, employees or teammates must believe that you care about them. Second, they have to believe in what you're teaching them. For me, that means I have to admit my mistakes as a coach and apologize for them. Even though I'm the head of the team, I'm not better than my players. Their share in the team's success is worth as much as mine. If I'm not living out what I'm preaching to them, they'll never get it.

Teamwork is also about showing equal amounts of respect to every member of the team. Steven Soderberg, a fellow University High alum and successful film director, once said in an interview, "On a movie set, there's a clear chain of command, but there's no chain of respect." What an amazing statement about teamwork! It doesn't matter who is on that set. Everybody gets an equal amount of respect from everyone, whether it's the lead actor, director, executive producer, stunt coordinator or janitor. Everyone should be equally respected.

This truth is beautifully illustrated in James 2:2-4: "Suppose someone comes into your meeting wearing a gold ring and fine clothes, and a poor person in filthy old clothes also comes in. If you show special attention to the one wearing fine clothes and say, 'Here's a good seat for you,' but say to the one who is poor, 'You stand there' or 'Sit on the floor by my feet,' have you not discriminated among yourselves and become judges with evil thoughts?" (*TNIV*).

Everybody should have equal value. God sees us all the same. There are no levels to God's love, and there are no levels of approval that can be earned in God's eyes. If God sees me the same as He sees the next guy, then how can I show favoritism in my leadership?

Jesus exemplified teamwork and love for others throughout His life on earth. He even loved and died for the very men who put those nails through His hands and His feet. Certainly Jesus knew He was going to be in that position. If that's the case, then there must have been a discussion about how it was going to happen. Can you imagine God drawing up that game plan? "Here's the game plan for Friday night," God in essence told Jesus. "You're going to get nailed to a cross and have a spear put through your side."

There's no greater example of someone giving it all for the team. If Jesus was willing to do that for us, then I, as a coach, have to be willing to lay it on the line for my players. The most I can give is a small fraction of what Jesus did on the cross. Our sinful nature is in direct contrast to that. Sin is selfishness. But love is about selflessness. Teamwork is the essence of love.

TRAINING TIME

1. What does "giving it all for the team" mean to you?
2. What are some of the difficulties you face as a leader when it comes to favoritism and how you treat those you are leading?

3. Accountability, selflessness and love are key elements of teamwork. Which attributes do you need to exemplify more fully so you can be better equipped to teach the concept of teamwork?

PRAYER

Father, as I lead others, help me to embrace the power of Christlike love for everyone. I want to give myself up for the greater cause, to see Your kingdom built up and to help those I am leading fulfill the calling You have for them.

Brian Kinchen is a retired NFL tight end and long snapper who was a member of the 2003 Super Bowl champion New England Patriots. In his 13 years in the NFL, he also played for Miami, Cleveland, Baltimore and Carolina. Kinchen, a graduate of Louisiana State University, is currently the head varsity football coach at Ascension Christian High School in Gonzales, Louisiana.

See the Big Picture

JUSTIN MASTERSON
MLB Pitcher

Leading with clarity requires an eternal perspective.

I'm a competitor. My job is to play a game. If someone were to watch me throughout a season, they would know that every single time I go out on the mound, I give the best I have on that day. When people talk to me, they see this laid-back guy who's just having a good time—who's just happy to be here. And yet, after they see me on the mound, they say, "Man, you're ferocious!" or "You're not afraid to pitch to anyone!" Sometimes they ask, "How do you do it?"

It's really simple: I want to do my best. I want to win. If you give me a task to complete, I'm going to do everything I can to complete it to the best of my ability. In order to continue to perform at that level day after day, you can't dwell on what happened in the past. If something bad happens and you stay focused on it, that leads to an inability to move on and live the life the Lord has given you.

In other words, it's all about seeing the big picture. If I don't have a clear understanding of God's purpose for my life and the ultimate reason for my existence, then I'm not going to be effective as an athlete, as a leader in the clubhouse, or as a Christian who hopes to have influence in this world.

One thing I must always remember is that my life as a baseball player is fleeting. I could have awakened today, maybe slept on my arm wrong, and never been able to pitch again. If I'm not okay with that, then for me, that would be a problem. Not that I don't want to play anymore, but there are many more important things to me than the game of baseball. There are my faith in God and my relationship with my wife, just to give a couple of examples. We don't know what the future holds, so we should appreciate every day we're given to do the things God has gifted us to do.

Seeing the big picture allows us to understand that we can't walk this journey of faith alone. Fellowship is key. Otherwise, it's easy to feel like you're alone—like you're the only Christian. You can start falling into wrong paths and not notice it. When I'm pitching, I can't always see what I'm doing wrong. I don't have the right perspective. Coaches and players who are watching me can see things I can't see. I take that same concept into my daily walk with Christ. I need another set of eyes. I need someone I can talk to and who will help me to keep going in the right direction.

When I see the big picture, I realize there's nothing I can do without the Lord. I'm constantly encouraged by my favorite verse, Philippians 4:13: "I am able to do all things through Him who strengthens me." That Scripture has been such a revelation for me. As Paul wrote that, he was in his weakest time physically. He wasn't talking about how he could lift a heavy boulder or perform an amazing feat. Paul was making the transparent admission that in his weakest state, Christ was there to strengthen him.

Seeing the big picture also means understanding that I'm here for a reason and, right now, that means being called to be a light to the baseball community. I'm not going to jump up in a teammate's face and tell him he's going to hell. It's more about my lifestyle. I'm trying to live out what Jesus has called me to do. It's about taking the opportunities I'm given to share with people why I'm so happy and how my life is so much better because Christ is in it. It's the Holy Spirit who's going to do the work in people's hearts. You build up your own relationship with Christ, and then you wait for the chance to minister. I love Matthew 22:37-39, because Jesus tells us, plain and simple, to "love the Lord your God with all your heart, with all your soul, and with all your mind," and to "love your neighbor as yourself."

Having an eternal perspective is vitally important. We must understand that this life is all about leading others to relationship with Christ. Nothing else really matters if we're not living out the Great Commission that Jesus gave us (see Matthew 28:18-20). Christ's leadership shows us that He was all about that eternal perspective. He was sent to earth for a very specific purpose. Yes, He came to show us how to live a life that glorifies God. But first and foremost, He came to die on the cross for our sins so that we might spend eternity in heaven with Him. That's why Jesus was able to go through pain and suffering even to His death.

As a leader, I want to have the same eternal perspective that drove Christ to fulfill His purpose. I want to maintain a clear view of the big picture and not allow the small, insignificant things of this life to distract me from that mission.

TRAINING TIME

1. What does seeing the big picture mean to you in your personal life or in your life as a leader?
2. What are some of the "small, insignificant things" that sometimes distract you from seeing the big picture or the more important goals that you want to accomplish?

3. Moving forward, what are some ways that you might be able to keep an eternal perspective at the forefront of everything you do?

PRAYER

Father, give me an eternal perspective that focuses on Your mission. Help me resist the temptation to focus too closely on the details that have no bearing on my calling here on earth and no impact on eternity.

Justin Masterson is a starting pitcher for the Cleveland Indians. He began his career with the Boston Red Sox, where he was a part of two American League playoff teams. Masterson was the first Red Sox pitcher since 1912 to make his first four starts in Fenway Park and not lose any of them.

See the Future

CHARLIE WARD

Retired NBA Guard and Heisman Trophy Winner

Leading others requires a vision of where you're going.

Sometimes the words "dream" and "vision" are interchanged, but the two concepts are distinct. *Merriam Webster's Dictionary* defines the word "dream" as "a strongly desired goal or purpose," while "vision" can be defined as "unusual discernment or foresight."

We have our dreams and God has His vision. Sometimes following either brings us to the same place, but often God has a different vision for our lives than what we have in mind. While we might be passionate about our goals, we must have a vision or "unusual discernment" of what God wants for us.

As a leader, it's essential to understand the principle of vision and then to catch the vision that God has for your life. First of all, you need to have a relationship with the heavenly Father so that you can see His heart. Many times we try to live on our own merit, but when you have a relationship with God, you can always refer back to His plans.

Another key to discovering and walking in God's vision is allowing the influence of godly wisdom. Listen to what Christian mentors have to say and then make good decisions based on that counsel. God has blessed me with people whom I can trust and follow on my journey to His perfect will. If you don't already have those kinds of relationships in your life, I encourage you to seek them out.

As you start to see God's plan revealed, it's important to set goals and make them plain by writing them down and referring back to them often. Then make preparations for God to work in your life. That takes prayer and fasting and an attitude of expectation.

Early in my career with the New York Knicks, I spent two years playing alongside Monty Williams. We became good friends and remain close today. As his playing career was winding down, Monty had a desire to get into coaching. He started hanging around the San Antonio Spurs, and they gave him an opportunity to be a staff intern. His goals were simple: to learn, to help the players get better, and to be used by God. Then Monty was hired as an assistant with the Portland Trailblazers, where he spent five years.

It didn't take long for Monty's name to start surfacing as one of the top assistants in the league. Up to that point, his focus was to be content where God had him. Even though he wasn't actively seeking out a head coaching position, the New Orleans Hornets hired him in 2010. It was his time, and he was prepared.

Like Monty, I've always tried to be flexible and keep my options open. As a multi-sport athlete, that wasn't always easy to do. As my college career at Florida State was ending, I had the opportunity to play for the New York Yankees. I also had my eye on the NFL Draft. But as a senior, I committed myself to my basketball teammates and tried not to worry about those other possibilities.

As I focused on basketball, I made the decision to turn down the Yankees. I also missed out on a lot of the pre-draft football workouts that are so important. When the NFL Draft passed and I didn't get selected, I wasn't down and disappointed like others around me were. At that point, I realized a professional football career wasn't part of God's plan for my life. So I worked very hard for the NBA Draft, and God blessed me with an opportunity there.

The Bible provides a stark description of what happens when leaders don't have a grasp of God's vision for their lives and work. In Proverbs 29:18, Solomon plainly says, "Where there is no vision, the people perish" (*KJV*).

That verse reminds me of another good friend of mine who coached his children in basketball. When teaching them about defense, he always used to shout, "No vision! No vision!" He knew that if the opponent couldn't see, that lack of vision would cause turnovers and give his team an advantage.

When we allow distractions, obstacles and unforeseen circumstances to disrupt our vision, we will walk aimlessly, have no purpose and be unable to see past today. As a substitute for long-term vision, we will look for feel-good moments and end up doing things that do not please God. Those around us will suffer as a result of the consequences that come our way. Nothing but destruction follows a life with no vision.

The best way I know to avoid that scenario is to look to the leader who best understood and fulfilled God's vision. From the time man fell to sin, Jesus knew the plan to redeem the world. He understood that the purpose was so that all of us could have a relationship with the Father. He caught the vision. In His ministry, He always pointed towards His heavenly Father. Even though He prayed that the cup would pass from Him (see Matthew 26:39), He understood that there was a greater purpose.

As you search for God's vision in your life, you can rest in the knowledge that He has a singular vision for all who call Him Lord. We are to work to share our testimony with others. We as

Christian leaders have a common purpose to lead others into relationship with Jesus Christ. He has called us to live lives that are pleasing to Him and allow others to see Jesus living through us.

TRAINING TIME

1. What are some dreams you have for your life? How do those dreams line up with the vision that God has revealed to you thus far?
2. What steps have you taken to catch God's vision for your life?
3. How does Jesus' example inspire you to follow His vision until you've completed the task at hand?

PRAYER

Father, make my dreams and Your vision for my life one and the same. Reveal to me the distractions that hinder me from seeing that vision, and then give me the strength to overcome any obstacles that may get in my way.

Charlie Ward is a retired 11-year NBA veteran who played for the New York Knicks, San Antonio Spurs and Houston Rockets. At Florida State, he was the winner of seven major football awards, including the 1993 Heisman Trophy. Ward, a member of the College Football Hall of Fame, led the Seminoles to their first national title that same season. He is currently the head football coach at Westbury Christian School in Houston, Texas.

Follow First, then Lead

DANIEL SEPULVEDA

NFL Punter; Super Bowl Champion

Leaders must learn to sacrifice and follow Jesus.

The game of football is a great teacher. The lessons I've learned from playing football—hard work, sacrifice and teamwork—are applicable to the rest of my life. When I look at the principles at work in this game and in life, I've had the opportunity to learn something about leadership—but not in the way you'd expect.

Although the world will tell you that leaders must be out in front, at the top and before everyone else, Jesus teaches that in order to lead well, you must first lay down your life and learn to follow.

When we think of sacrifice in sports, we think of the blood, sweat and tears that go into preparation, and of the passionate application of that work on game day. We think these things are what make good football players great, and we are right. But the possibilities for a life dedicated to sacrifice go way beyond a legendary sporting career.

We "worship" our favorite athletes when they are victorious on the football field and look up to them as they model these positive attributes. These men sacrifice themselves for excellence. Is this a worthy calling? Absolutely! But I know someone who sacrificed Himself for far more than excellence. Jesus Christ, by His sacrificial leadership, redefined greatness for His followers and laid the framework for what it looks like to be a leader.

Jesus taught that if we want to be the greatest, we must serve others. Many great leaders have modeled this principle for me, and for that I am very grateful. The servant leadership that my father provided our family was my earliest experience of real leadership, and it made a great impact on me. I have often heard my dad speak about leadership. As the CEO of a major private company, he is often solicited to share with others what it means to lead. His four sons have benefited many times from that same wisdom.

"The first thing you need to know about leadership," my dad always says, "is that you cannot lead anyone until you learn how to follow." What does that mean? Even in leading yourself, you must be a follower. Sacrifice is required! Time, energy and effort must be spent pursuing a closer relationship with Jesus Christ. That investment will put you in a position to lead yourself and in turn lead others.

But the only way God can truly teach me about sacrifice is through my own life experience. God has blessed me tremendously. I never would have expected that my dreams of being a professional athlete would come true. I am very grateful for the blessings God has bestowed upon me. Thanks in part to my positive upbringing, I recognize that my time, talents and resources are not my own. When this realization settles in, it becomes apparent how important it is to lay down this life for the glory of God. So, in order to lead myself well, I first have to recognize the sacrifice that involves. I am not my own. I was bought at a price. At the root of leadership, even leadership of your own life, is sacrifice.

Stories of leadership are found throughout Scripture. There are examples of inspiring leadership through difficult times, and examples of judgment and exile that resulted, in large part, from poor leadership. Most often these poor leaders were caught up in their pride. In Ezekiel 34, God describes to His people through the prophet how Israel's leaders failed them through the years, resulting in their subsequent exile and captivity in Babylon. One of the principal reasons the Israelites could not adhere to the requirements of the Mosaic Law was poor leadership. In this case, the kings of Israel and Judah were selfish, proud, greedy and deceitful. Their most glaring failure, however, was not providing for the needs of their people. A leader, before anything else, must learn to serve.

On the other end of the spectrum, we have the example of Jesus, who not only cared for the needs of His disciples as they left their former lives behind, but also redefined leadership through His service to them when He washed their feet (see John 13:1-17). On the night before His death, in the midst of an argument about which disciple would be greatest in heaven—second to Jesus, of course—Jesus redefined leadership through His example and His declaration: "I am among you as the One who serves" (Luke 22:27). He asks us to serve one another as He has served us.

As Christians, we cannot ignore this glaring example of what it means to love and to serve. Jesus is the greatest leader ever because He loved better than any man ever has or ever will. He denied Himself and His desires in order to obey the will of His father, even to death.

So what are the benefits of servant leadership? What do I get when my primary focus is on serving others and denying my own interests? If life is ultimately about serving God, glorifying Him, and making choices that are consistent with His will for us, then how can we be at peace—real peace—if we're not doing those things? We can't—certainly not for a long period of time anyway. So the benefit of living a life of leadership through sacrifice is peace.

Knowing that you are making decisions that are pleasing to the God of the universe is a very reassuring thought. In fact, it should drive us. The very deepest parts of us should recognize the value of honoring God with our lives. When reality sets in, and the Spirit of God reveals this truth to our hearts in a compelling way, it becomes easier to lay down our lives for others.

On the other hand, if we ignore this truth or deny reality, then we are susceptible to the destructive power of pride. If we, for one minute, forget who we are, then we begin to buy into the message of the world that says, "You are the man!" My flesh likes to hear that. If I don't often remind myself that God is "the man" and I am not, I may start to believe what I'm hearing. So just as a life of peace comes from denying our desires for the sake of those whom we are leading, believing that we are powerful, significant and influential will lead to a life destroyed by pride.

Let's not compromise the best that God has in store for us by falling prey to pride in our position as leaders. Instead, let us pursue humility when we lead, and by so doing inspire those whom God has given us the opportunity to influence and guide.

TRAINING TIME

1. What is the greatest challenge in your quest to become a servant leader?
2. What are some things you may need to sacrifice in order to serve others in a more meaningful way?
3. Peace is one of the benefits of servant leadership. What do you think might be some other benefits?

PRAYER

*Father, reveal to me the attitudes and fears that distract me
from being a servant leader. Give me the strength and
determination to daily sacrifice my personal ambitions and
desires that stand in the way of Your perfect will for my life.*

Daniel Sepulveda is the punter for the Pittsburgh Steelers and was a member of the Super Bowl XLIII champion team. At Baylor University, he was a four-time All-Big-12 selection and three-time All-American. Sepulveda is the only college player to twice win the Ray Guy Award, given to the nation's best punter.

Do It for the Lord

KAY YOW

Legendary Women's Basketball Coach, North Carolina State University

---

Leading means accepting the call to excellence.

John Wooden is my coaching role model. His definition of success shaped me as a coach. He famously said, "Success is peace of mind that is a direct result of self-satisfaction in knowing you did your best to become the best that you are capable of becoming."

After his retirement, Coach Wooden modified that statement to include the role that God plays in our pursuit of excellence: "There is only one kind of life that truly succeeds, and that is the one that places faith in the hands of the Savior. Until that is done, we are on an aimless course that runs in circles and goes nowhere."

I wholeheartedly agree with Coach Wooden's definition of success. Success only comes as one pursues excellence.

The first thing that comes to mind when I think about excellence is the apostle Paul's words in Colossians 3:23-24, where he wrote, "Whatever you do, do it enthusiastically, as something done for the Lord and not for men, knowing that you will receive the reward of an inheritance from the Lord—you serve the Lord Christ."

The message is simple: Whatever you do, do it to glorify God. Use the talents and abilities He's given you to honor Him. If that's your motive, I fully know and believe with all my heart that God will guide and direct you and give you wisdom as you work towards a life of excellence.

Early in my coaching career, I started keeping a scrapbook. When reading the newspaper or a magazine, I would pay close attention to stories about highly successful people and make note of what they said about their keys to success. I would cut the articles out and put them in my notebook. They might come from a football coach like Joe Paterno or a basketball coach like John Wooden. I went back from time to time and read their quotations for inspiration.

By studying these coaches, I became convinced that teaching fundamentals is critical if you want to be successful in the sports field. You have to learn the fundamentals. As time went by, it was exciting for me to begin to connect some of the dots between what these people were saying and what God was saying.

For example, when people asked me what the key to athletic success was, I always picked the word "attitude." But attitude is also a key to successful living. You'll quickly realize this if you study Jesus' attitude in all of the situations He faced and how He responded. Soon I was no longer just trying to understand excellence in the field of sports; it had become equally important to pursue excellence through a life guided by Jesus' example. He was the epitome of excellence, and to me, excellence is all about glorifying God.

That brings us back to Colossians 3:23-24. If you do things as unto God rather than unto men, and if you give everything from your heart, soul and mind, then you're going to work hard. This is the cornerstone of success, and it's going to come naturally because you're doing it out of love for the Lord. Your motivation will always be love.

As a coach, you want your players to strive for excellence, and you do so by encouraging them. Of course you have to correct, but as Warren Wiersbe said, "Truth without love is brutality, and love without truth is hypocrisy." You cannot love without truth. You've got to tell people the truth to help them move to a higher level. But if you give the truth without love, it becomes very cold.

Having the correct attitude and maintaining character allows you the opportunity to speak truth. It gives you the authority to tell your team members what they need to do to pursue excellence. People see me and think I'm coaching basketball. But I think I'm coaching people. If you become a winner as a person, you will have your best chance to win on the court. People without character always fall short of excellence. No matter how talented they are or what great players they may be, they will fall short. They will fail you when you need them the most.

On the other hand, players who have the right attitude and pure motives will achieve their potential and be there when you need them. That's one of the special blessings of coaching. It's such a reward. We get so many awards in athletics, but I've always treasured the rewards—those benefits we receive on the inside—so much more. Awards get tarnished. You lose them. You break them. But the rewards you keep forever. Seeing your players start to understand the true meaning of excellence is one of those rewards. You know that they've taken a great step forward in life.

In studying excellence, I've learned that many of us are more concerned about the end result or the production from our efforts. We can easily forget about the process. This is where all the learning takes place. We don't always see the big picture. We see more of the short term. Success often equals money or position or power or a title. Yet, if someone hasn't given his or her very best and hasn't gone about things the right way, then that's not excellence. Some people will step on others to get what they want. But there are no shortcuts to true excellence. A commitment to doing it the right way is just as much a part of excellence as anything else.

As Coach Wooden said, knowing Jesus as your personal Lord and Savior is the difference. You can do many things well and become successful in the eyes of the world, but you can't live successfully without knowing Him and without having Him at the center of your life. Pursuing Jesus is what makes a life excellent.

TRAINING TIME

1. What is your definition of success and how have you seen it (or how do you hope to see it) manifested in your life?
2. The pursuit of excellence requires a heavy dose of truth and love. What are some examples of how experiencing God's truth in a loving manner paves the way to excellence?
3. Do you agree that excellence is "about the journey"? Why or why not?

PRAYER

Father, give me a desire to pursue excellence.
Create in me a heart with pure motives and the ability to
accept Your perfect truth and love along the way.

Kay Yow was the women's basketball coach at North Carolina State for 34 years, during which she led the Wolfpack women to five ACC regular season championships, four ACC Tournament titles, 20 NCAA Tournaments, five AIAW Tournaments and two NIT appearances. In 38 seasons as a head coach, she compiled a career 737-344 record. Yow coached the U.S. Olympic team to the 1988 gold medal and is a member of both the Women's Basketball and Naismith Memorial Basketball Halls of Fame. This chapter was created using excerpts from an interview that FCA conducted with Kay Yow on April 28, 2008 for the book *Serving*. Coach Yow passed away nine months later, on January 24, 2009, after a lengthy battle against breast cancer.

The Greatest Leader Ever

MILES McPHERSON

Pastor and Founder, The Rock Church, San Diego

Leading like Christ is the only way to lead.

Historically, I believe that Dr. Martin Luther King Jr. was the greatest Christian leader of our time. He put his reputation, his physical well-being, his personal freedom and his very life on the line for a battle in which victory was anything but certain. Despite the incredible obstacles he and his followers faced, Dr. King was fully committed to the mission God gave him.

As Dr. King did in so many ways, all Christian leaders need to lead like Jesus. Whether our leadership role is as a parent, an employer, a community servant, an athlete, a coach or a minister, the only way we can fulfill what He's called us to do is to do it His way.

On a personal level, I've seen effective Christian leadership in the form of my first pastor, Mike MacIntosh, at Horizon Christian Fellowship in San Diego. He inspired me and gave me vision. He showed me what is possible when you mobilize people for ministry. Pastor MacIntosh gave me the opportunity to do things I didn't think I was ready to do. His example is one I still follow today.

There are numerous qualities that an effective leader must embody. You've already read about some in the previous chapters of this book. I will highlight here a few principles that are particularly important.

First, *effective leaders must be gifted to lead.* Some people aren't upfront leaders. That doesn't mean they're not important or valuable; they're just better in supporting roles. Potential leaders need to understand to what degree they need to lead and at what point they need to follow more gifted or experienced leaders. They need to know their place in the leadership spectrum.

Second, *effective leaders must have a vision.* Great leaders can see the future—not in the sense that they can predict upcoming events, but true leaders have a vision for what needs to be accomplished and can see that before others do. Then, as they move towards that vision, they need to be willing to take risks for what they believe. They need to be very committed to the vision.

Third, *effective leaders must be secure.* Good leaders know who they are and understand how they fit in the grand scheme of things. They can comfortably encourage other people to step out and join them in leadership. When the right time comes, they aren't afraid to turn the reigns over to those they have trained and mentored.

Fourth, *effective leaders must have a servant's heart.* Leaders should always encourage and empower other people to do more than they think they can do. That requires serving those they are leading by speaking to their weakness, hesitation and self-doubt, and encouraging them to believe in the gifts and calling God has given them. That is what servant leadership looks like.

While I've learned these key principles from the greatest leader in my personal life, Pastor MacIntosh, and the greatest leader of our time, Dr. King, nothing can compare to what Jesus

Christ, the greatest leader ever, can teach us.

Jesus had countless followers during His short time on earth and has since been the focus of admiration and discipleship for billions of people. With that in mind, let's take a look at these four key principles again, but this time through the lens of Christ's example:

First, Jesus was gifted to lead. As the "firstborn over all creation" (Colossians 1:15), He came to do something that had never been done before. He came to die for our sins and rise from the dead. But first, Jesus knew that He was going to have to equip 12 men to take the message to the world. He had to lead them for three and a half years in such a way that He could leave and trust them to carry on His work—and thereby change the world.

Second, Jesus had a vision. He saw the big picture. In Acts 1:8, just before He left the earth, He told the disciples, "But you will receive power when the Holy Spirit has come upon you, and you will be My witnesses in Jerusalem, in all Judea and Samaria, and to the ends of the earth." Even though they couldn't yet fathom the vision, Jesus knew that His disciples would take the gospel to the world. Even though Peter started out as a loose cannon, Jesus knew this fisherman would turn into a mighty man of God and become the cornerstone or "rock" upon which His church would be built.

Third, Jesus was secure. In Matthew 4:1-11, we read about Satan's efforts to tempt Him to prove who He was. Jesus didn't take the bait. Leading up to His crucifixion, He was arrested and beaten by men who challenged His word. Even though He could have stopped it at any moment, He submitted Himself to the punishment. Why? Because He was secure in knowing His role in a cause that was bigger and more important than His personal comfort or safety.

Fourth, Jesus had a servant's heart. Jesus gave up His place in heaven to become a man and to live as a servant for the sake of our salvation. As we read in Philippians 2:8, "He humbled Himself by becoming obedient to the point of death—even to death on a cross." Just a few days earlier, Jesus had washed His disciples' feet—an act of service He performed not just literally, but also metaphorically by discipling them, equipping them and entrusting them with a mission that was bigger than their individual lives.

Yes, Jesus is far and above the greatest leader ever. He set a perfect example of service. He didn't feel the need to defend Himself. He went through with His plan even though He knew He would be attacked.

I'm so thankful that I have benefited from Jesus' personal investment in my life through His Holy Spirit. He's encouraged me. He's helped me lay my life down for others. He's given me the courage to commit to the cause that He's put in my heart. He's shown me how to stay the course even when it's hard—and when it gets hard, He reminds me of what He went through and that it's a privilege to be persecuted for His name's sake.

Unfortunately, many leaders fail to follow the leadership principles of Christ. If you don't lead like Jesus, you're leading like yourself. Doing things for yourself eventually brings death. That kind of leadership is based on selfishness and leads to self-destruction. Even worse, it will also lead those following you down a path of destruction.

If you're like me and many other Christian leaders around the world who want to lead like Christ, there are some important things you must understand. First, you need to know what your leadership is supposed to accomplish. Your goal should be to lead Christ followers; therefore, you need to be a Christ follower.

Next, you need to understand that there is a spiritual component to your leadership. It's not just about forming and executing strategies. It's about the Holy Spirit guiding and directing you—and doing work in people's hearts and lives that you cannot accomplish. You need to be submitted to Christ for Christ's glory and not your own.

Finally, your leadership is to build God's kingdom. Your goal needs to be to help people live holy lives and become Christ followers. That should be the ultimate standard for successful leadership: helping people enter a relationship with Jesus Christ.

None of this can happen until you've taken the first big step. Leading like Christ starts with having a relationship with Christ. It's not about head knowledge; it's a heart experience. In order to have that relationship, you need to surrender your heart and your life to Him. It's through your relationship with Him that Christ is going to guide and direct you to lead like He did. It's through that relationship that you're going to begin to think like Jesus, and then have the power to lead like Jesus.

If you've been in relationship with Christ, but you've gotten cold or lost your way, you need to ask yourself some hard questions. What is the fruit of your life? Do you have joy? Do you have vision? Do you have patience? Do you have the fruit of the Spirit (see Galatians 5:22-23) in your life? As you realize how much you are lacking, you'll be reminded of the abundance that you experienced when your relationship with Christ was active and intimate.

Once you commit (or recommit) to Christ, you are saying no to yourself. You are giving up how you used to lead and how you once saw the people who follow you. Surrendering to Him is step one in the process of abandoning your way of doing things and adopting Christ's way of doing things.

Only then will you supernaturally inherit the opportunity to accomplish bigger things for Jesus, because He will know that you're going to handle those things in ways that honor Him. By His strength, you will be able to do things beyond your own abilities. You will learn to lead with the power of Jesus Christ.

TRAINING TIME

1. Have you ever made the decision to commit your life fully to Jesus Christ by accepting His free gift of salvation?
2. Read the following verses and think about what each one means to you personally: Romans 3:23; Romans 6:23; Romans 5:8; 1 Corinthians 15:3-6; John 3:16; John 14:6; 2 Corinthians 7:10; John 1:12; John 5:24; Romans 10:9-13.
3. If you have never made a commitment to Jesus Christ, are you willing to repent and receive Him as Lord of your life? If so, express to God your need for Him. Consider using the suggested prayer of commitment below. Remember that God is more concerned with your attitude than with the words you say.

PRAYER

Lord Jesus, I need You. I realize I'm a sinner, and I can't save myself. I need Your forgiveness. I believe that You loved me so much that You died on the cross for my sins and rose from the dead. I repent of my sins and put my faith in You as Savior and Lord. Take control of my life and help me to follow You in obedience. I love You, Jesus. In Your name, amen.

Miles McPherson is a published author, motivational speaker, and the pastor and founder of The Rock Church in San Diego. Before entering the ministry, he spent four years as a defensive back with the San Diego Chargers. McPherson played collegiately at the University of New Haven, where he was the school's first All-American.

ACKNOWLEDGMENTS

Special thanks to the editorial team of Chad Bonham, Shea Vailes, Alexis Spencer-Byers and Anna Lile. Special thanks to the Regal Publishing team for believing in this project; Steven Lawson, for making sure it became reality; and the FCA leadership: Les Steckel, Tom Rogeberg, Ken Williams, Nancy Hedrick and Donnie Dee. Contributor thanks to Jeremy Affeldt, San Francisco Giants; Jane Albright, University of Nevada—Reno; Shaun Alexander; Tony Bennett and Rich Murray, University of Virginia; Lance Berkman and Melody Yount, St. Louis Cardinals; Tamika Catchings, Catch a Star Foundation; Michael Chang and Caroline Nakata, Chang Family Foundation; Jean Driscoll; Steve Fitzhugh; Maurice Foxworth, Innovation Works; Ryan Hall; Clint Hurdle and Jim Trdinich, Pittsburgh Pirates; Mike Jarvis, Florida Atlantic University; Avery Johnson, Heather Huppert and Gary Sussman, New Jersey Nets; Clark Kellogg and David Benner, Indiana Pacers; Jackie Joyner-Kersee and Angela Roberson, Jackie Joyner-Kersee Foundation; Clayton and Ellen Kershaw and Ann Higginbottom, Los Angeles Dodgers; Brian Kinchen; Jerry Kindall; David Daly, FCA Baseball; Chris Klein, Los Angeles Galaxy; Kyle Korver, Chicago Bulls; Karlton Korver, Seer Outfitters; Tom Landry Jr. and Rick Bowles; Justin Masterson and Bart Swain, Cleveland Indians; Bruce Matthews and Robbie Bohren, Tennessee Titans; Miles McPherson and Seneca Hampton, The Rock Church, San Diego; Madeline Manning-Mims; Tom Osborne and Anne Hackbart, University of Nebraska; Andy Pettitte; Lorenzo Romar and Jamee Ashburn, University of Washington; Jim Ryun, Anne Ryun and Ned Ryun; Sue Semrau, Melissa Bruner and David Schmidt, Florida State University; Daniel Sepulveda, Pittsburgh Steelers; Teddi Domann, Domann & Pittman Football; John Shelby and Mike Vassallo,

Milwaukee Brewers; Mike Singletary, Tom West and Bob Hagan, Minnesota Vikings; Charlie Ward, Westbury Christian School; Kurt Warner and Jen Zink, First Things First Foundation; Pat Williams and Andrew Herdliska, Orlando Magic; the family of John Wooden; Danny Wuerffel and Sara Pace, Desire Street Ministries; Marsha Sharp, Kay Yow Cancer Fund; and Stephanie Glance.

FELLOWSHIP OF CHRISTIAN ATHLETES COACH'S MANDATE

Pray as though nothing of eternal value is going
to happen in my athletes' lives unless God does it.

Prepare each practice and game as giving "my utmost for His highest."

Seek not to be served by my athletes for personal gain, but seek
to serve them as Christ served the church.

Be satisfied not with producing a good record, but with producing good athletes.

Attend carefully to my private and public walk with God, knowing that the
athlete will never rise to a standard higher than that being lived by the coach.

Exalt Christ in my coaching, trusting the Lord will then draw athletes to Himself.

Desire to have a growing hunger for God's Word, for personal
obedience, for fruit of the spirit and for saltiness in competition.

Depend solely upon God for transformation—one athlete at a time.

Preach Christ's word in a Christ-like demeanor, on and off the field of competition.

Recognize that it is impossible to bring glory to both myself
and Christ at the same time.

Allow my coaching to exude the fruit of the Spirit,
thus producing Christ-like athletes.

Trust God to produce in my athletes His chosen purposes,
regardless of whether the wins are readily visible.

Coach with humble gratitude, as one privileged to be God's coach.

Fellowship of Christian Athletes Competitor's Creed

I am a Christian first and last.
I am created in the likeness of God Almighty to bring Him glory.
I am a member of Team Jesus Christ.
I wear the colors of the cross.

I am a Competitor now and forever.
I am made to strive, to strain, to stretch and to succeed in the arena of competition.
I am a Christian Competitor and as such, I face my challenger with the face of Christ.

I do not trust in myself.
I do not boast in my abilities or believe in my own strength.
I rely solely on the power of God.
I compete for the pleasure of my Heavenly Father, the honor
of Christ and the reputation of the Holy Spirit.

My attitude on and off the field is above reproach—my conduct beyond criticism.
Whether I am preparing, practicing or playing,
I submit to God's authority and those He has put over me.
I respect my coaches, officials, teammates, and competitors out of respect for the Lord.

My body is the temple of Jesus Christ.
I protect it from within and without.
Nothing enters my body that does not honor the Living God.
My sweat is an offering to my Master. My soreness is a sacrifice to my Savior.

I give my all—all the time.
I do not give up. I do not give in. I do not give out.
I am the Lord's warrior—a competitor by conviction and a disciple of determination.
I am confident beyond reason because my confidence lies in Christ.
The results of my effort must result in His glory.

Let the competition begin.
Let the glory be God's.

Sign the Creed • Go to www.fca.org
© 2011 FCA.

Impacting the World for Christ Through Sports

Since 1954, the Fellowship of Christian Athletes has challenged athletes and coaches to impact the world for Jesus Christ. FCA is cultivating Christian principles in local communities nationwide by encouraging, equipping and empowering others to serve as examples and make a difference. Reaching approximately 2 million people annually on the professional, college, high school, junior high and youth levels, FCA has grown into the largest Christian sports ministry in the world. Through FCA's Four Cs of Ministry—Coaches, Campus, Camps and Community—and the shared passion for athletics and faith, lives are changed for current and future generations.

FCA'S FOUR Cs OF MINISTRY

Coaches: Coaches are the heart of FCA. Our role is to minister to them by encouraging and equipping them to know and serve Christ. FCA ministers to coaches through Bible studies, prayer support, discipleship and mentoring, resources, outreach events and retreats. FCA values coaches, first for who they are, and for what God has created them to do.

Campus: The Campus Ministry is initiated and led by student-athletes and coaches on junior high, high school, and college campuses. The Campus Ministry types—Huddles, Team Bible Studies, Chaplain Programs and Coaches Bible Studies—are effective ways to establish FCA ministry presence, as well as outreach events such as One Way 2 Play–Drug Free programs, school assemblies and Fields of Faith.

Camp: Camp is a time of "inspiration and perspiration" for coaches and athletes to reach their potential by offering comprehensive athletic, spiritual and leadership training. FCA offers seven types of camps: Sports Camps, Leadership Camps, Coaches Camps, Power Camps, Partnership Camps, Team Camps and International Camps.

Community: FCA has ministries that reach the community through partnerships with local churches, businesses, parents and volunteers. These ministries not only reach out to the community, but also allow the community to invest in athletes and coaches. Non-school-based sports, adult ministries, youth sports, FCA Teams, clinics, resources and professional athlete ministries are the areas of Community Ministry.

VISION

To see the world impacted for Jesus Christ through the influence of athletes and coaches.

MISSION

To present to athletes and coaches, and all whom they influence, the challenge and adventure of receiving Jesus Christ as Savior and Lord, serving Him in their relationships and in the fellowship of the Church.

VALUES

Integrity • Serving • Teamwork • Excellence

Fellowship of Christian Athletes

8701 Leeds Road • Kansas City, MO 64129
www.fca.org • fca@fca.org • 1-800-289-0909
COMPETITORS FOR CHRIST

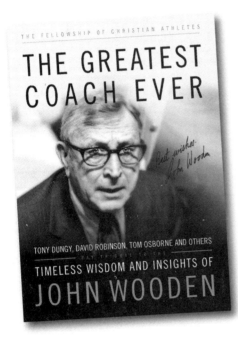